PSYCHOLOGICAL EVALUATION
OF
EXCEPTIONAL CHILDREN

PSYCHOLOGICAL EVALUATION OF EXCEPTIONAL CHILDREN

By

HAROLD D. LOVE, Ed.D.

Professor of Special Education
University of Central Arkansas
Conway, Arkansas

CHARLES C THOMAS • PUBLISHER
Springfield • Illinois • U.S.A.

Published and Distributed Throughout the World by

CHARLES C THOMAS • PUBLISHER
2600 South First Street
Springfield, Illinois 62717

© *1985 by* CHARLES C THOMAS • PUBLISHER

ISBN 0-398-05045-7

Library of Congress Catalog Card Number: 84-8593

Printed in the United States of America
Q-R-3

Library of Congress Cataloging in Publication Data

Love, Harold D.
  Psychological evaluation of exceptional children.

  Includes index.
  1. Psychological tests for children. 2. Handicapped
children — Testing. 3. Child psychopathology — Diagnosis. 4. Handicapped children — Education. 5. Handicapped children — Education — Law and legislation —
United States. I. Title.
RJ503.5.L68   1984   155.4'5   84-8593
ISBN 0-398-05045-7

PREFACE

PSYCHOLOGICAL Evaluation of Exceptional Children has been prepared during a time of unusually rapid evolution and change in the field of special education and regular education. Of particular importance is the fact that education now must be free, appropriate to each student's needs, and is a matter of federal mandate. Public Law 94-142, the Education for All Handicapped Children Act of 1975, dictates what has just been mentioned, and further states that the education must be provided within the most normal environment consistent with the student's needs. There must be appropriateness of evaluation and educational programming. Both the local and state educational agencies are held accountable for providing the best possible program for each handicapped child.

In order to plan an effective program the most important thing is to have a collection of a wide range of information about the child. This book represents effective evaluation and programming that each teacher should know about. Assessment must be planned properly and truly be individualized for each child. This text is intended to serve as an introduction to the topic of psychological evaluation for exceptional children. It is intended for the practitioner who will administer some of the simpler tests and to utilize the results of a variety of assessment information.

This text was prepared for teachers and administrators who are presently teaching and who will be there in the near future.

CONTENTS

PSYCHOLOGICAL EVALUATION
OF
EXCEPTIONAL CHILDREN

CHAPTER 1

ASSESSMENT: AN OVERVIEW

DURING elementary and secondary school we have all taken tests. We took tests to measure our scholastic aptitude or intelligence or to evaluate the extent to which we had benefited from instruction. We took commercially produced and teacher made tests. We took well standardized, poorly standardized and tests which were not standardized at all. Some of us took personality tests, interest tests and tests for vocational placement. Some students today as in past years take civil service tests or tests of specific skills like typing or manual dexterity. People who were drafted or enlisted in the Armed Forces took a battery of tests. Enrolling in college meant undergoing entrance examinations such as American College Testing (ACT) or Scholastic Aptitude Tests (SAT). Those people who decided to go to graduate school had to take aptitude, ability and English usage tests; those who became teachers had to take the National Teacher Examination (NTE).

Physicians, lawyers, engineers, psychologists, real estate agents and others must take tests to decide their competence to practice.

Teachers, guidance counselors, psychologists, social workers and school administrators will be required to take, administer and interpret tests all of their professional lives. Professional school personnel need a working knowledge of the important facets of testing. They need to know how to select the right test for the right situation and if the test is adequately standardized.

Assessing the intelligence and special abilities of children and adults is a complex, demanding, and yet rewarding activity. The clinician must have a variety of skills and talents including the

3

ability to work with children, adolescents and adults.

Many of these skills can be learned and this book will provide much valuable information to provide the clinician the tools to become a better provider of assessment. The author's use of the word *clinician* refers to a number of professionals, among them clinical psychologists, school psychologists, educational psychologists, special educators, guidance counselors and speech pathologists. Occasionally, physicians and social workers use some of the tests and techniques discussed in this text.

The following, according to Sattler (1982, pp. 3-4), are important guidelines which should be followed in using intelligence and special ability tests:

1. Tests are samples of behavior.
2. Tests do not reveal traits or capacities directly.
3. Tests purporting to measure a particular ability or skill should have adequate reliability and validity.
4. Test results should be interpreted in light of the child's cultural background, primary language, and handicapping conditions.
5. Test scores and other test performances may be affected by temporary states of fatigue, anxiety, or stress; by basic disturbances in personality; or by brain damage.
6. Tests purporting to measure the same ability may provide different scores for that ability.
7. Test results should be interpreted in relationship to other behaviors and to case history information; test results should never be interpreted in isolation.
8. Test results are dependent on the child's cooperation and motivation.

TESTING: DECLINE OR UPSURGE?

During the last ten years the question of whether testing has declined has been raised repeatedly in special education settings. Swanson and Watson (1982) state that many educators and psychologists have suggested a marked decline in test use and an increase in skepticism about their ability. They cite several researchers who believe this — among them are Bersoff (1973), Cleveland (1976), Crawford (1979), Scott (1980) and Smith and Knoff (1981). Swanson and Watson (1982, p. 7) state the reasons given for the decline are:

(1) disappointing research findings, (2) irrelevance to remediation, (3) skepticism about traits and personality characteristics, (4) state and national laws restricting the use of testing, and (5) poor academic preparation in the use of tests.

This author believes that there has been an increase in evaluation because of P.L. 94-142. Before P.L. 94-142 was passed the Education Amendments Act (P.L. 93-380) was approved by Congress in 1974. This act guaranteed among other things, assurance of nondiscriminatory assessment, assurance of due process and assurance of education in the least restrictive setting. About a year later P.L. 94-142, the Education of All Handicapped Children Act, was signed into law by the president and strengthened the rights initially guaranteed by P.L. 93-380. P.L. 94-142 committed the federal government to huge financial allocations to the states meeting the requirements of the law and also, this act was not given an expiration date.

P.L. 94-142 mandates fair and appropriate testing of children between the ages of three and twenty-one years of age. Anyone testing children for placement in special education settings should be familiar with this section as it applies to the individual psychometric evaluation of children. The provisions of the law mandate a number of procedural requirements which must be met. They are:

1. Tests and other evaluation materials are administered in the child's native language or other mode of communication, unless it is clearly not feasible to do so;
2. The tests have been validated for the specific purpose for which they are used; and
3. The tests are administered by trained personnel in conformance with the instructions provided by their producer.

Interpretation, Number One (1). The child must be able to understand and respond to the examiner. For example, a child whose primary language is Spanish will be greatly discriminated against if tested by an examiner who only speaks English and will be further discriminated against if administered a test which did not use Spanish speaking children in its standardization procedure.

Interpretation, Number Two (2). An intelligence test must measure intelligence, an academic achievement test must measure achievement in various academic areas and compare children of one age with children of the same age. In other words, a test must measure what it purports to measure.

Interpretation, Number Three (3). Some tests can be given only by licensed psychologists, other tests can be administered by psychological examiners and still others can be administered by counselors, special educators, social workers, etc. The person giving the tests should be thoroughly familiar with the instructions, should have practiced administering the tests if inexperienced and should know something about the standardization procedure of the tests.

NONDISCRIMINATORY OR NONBIASED EVALUATION

A major dilemma which has faced special educators in the past and still faces us today relates to assessment which can be considered nonbiased or nondiscriminatory. We know that measurement of individual differences is designed to discriminate, but as Gearheart and Willenberg (1980, p. 7) say, "it should not discriminate against individuals because of racial, or socioeconomic background."

Public Law 94-142 lists the following statements under the section "Protection in Evaluation Procedures":

Testing and evaluation materials and procedures used for the purposes of evaluation and placement of handicapped children must be selected and administered so as not to be racially or culturally discriminatory.

State and local educational agencies shall insure, at a minimum, that:

(a) Tests and other evaluation materials:

    (1) Are provided and administered in the child's native language or other mode of communication, unless it is clearly not feasible to do so;

    (2) Have been validated for the specific purpose for which they are used; and

    (3) Are administered by trained personnel in conformance with the instructions provided by their producer;

(b) Tests and other evaluation materials include those tailored to assess specific areas of educational need and not merely those which are designed to provide a single intelligence quotient;

(c) Tests are selected and administered so as to best insure that when a test is administered to a child with impaired sensory, manual, or speaking skills, the test results accurately reflect the child's aptitude or achievement level or whatever other factors the test purports to measure, rather than reflecting the child's impaired sensory, manual, or speaking skills (except where those skills are the factors which the test purports to measure);

(d) No single procedure is used as the sole criterion for determining an appropriate educational program for a child; and

(e) The evaluation is made by a multidisciplinary team or group of persons including at least one teacher or other specialist with knowledge in the area of suspected disability.

(f) The child is assessed in all areas related to the suspected disability, including, where appropriate, health, vision, hearing, social and emotional status, general intelligence, academic performance, communicative status, and motor abilities.

In interpreting evaluation data and in making placement decisions, each public agency shall draw upon information from a variety of sources, including aptitude and achievement tests, teacher recommendations, physical condition, social or cultural background, and adaptive behavior.

The Council for Exceptional Children published in its journal *Exceptional Children* (1977) brief but specific suggestions that are not a part of the Rules and Regulations section of PL 94-142. They are presented here:

Policy Regarding Nondiscriminatory Evaluation

PL-94-142 requires that the manner by which testing and evaluation materials are selected and the procedures that are developed for evaluating handicapped children are to be free of racial or cultural overtones. The proposed regulations for Section 504 of the Vocational Rehabilitation Act of 1973 also require an individualized evaluation before educational placement decisions are made for handicapped persons. Consequently, the following policy is provided for consideration:

Nondiscriminatory Provisions

For the purposes of developing an individualized education program for each child, the local, intermediate, or state education agency shall establish procedures requiring nondiscriminatory testing and evaluation practices.

- Assessment instruments shall be appropriately adapted when used with children of impaired sensory, physical, or speaking skills and must consider each child's age and socioeconomic and cultural background.
- Specialists implementing evaluation procedures must be familiar with local cultural, language, and social patterns and practices.
- Tests and similar evaluation materials shall be administered in the child's primary language, wherever appropriate.

- Interpreters, in the native language and/or sign language, may be used throughout all phases of the evaluation.
- All communication with parents and the child shall be in the native language of the home.
- Local community norms shall be established when norm referenced tests are used.
- Criterion referenced instruments should be used.
- Developmental checklist(s) should be used where appropriate.
- Instruments shall be administered only by trained personnel according to the producer's instructions.
- Instruments shall assess specific abilities, not merely produce a single IQ score.
- No one result shall determine placement.

Public Law 94-142 and the suggestions by the Council for Exceptional Children in 1977 make it clear that assessment procedures must be fair and appropriate for the purposes of evaluation.

CONTROLLING THE QUALITY OF TESTS

This dilemma primarily relates to tests administered, those who administer them, the level of training of the examiner, certification requirements, ability of professional personnel and a host of other factors. Many of these factors will be controlled by the various states through the state departments of education, special education division. Many states have licensure laws for educational and psychological examiners and the people who obtain a license must pass rigid tests after years of appropriate education.

One problem which still remains with us concerns the competence of the committee members in the state departments of education in our country who chose the tests which are to be administered to children who receive special services. This is a greater problem, this author thinks, than the one involving the competency of the evaluators. This problem is not going to be solved any time soon and the real pity is that many people who select the tests which are to be administered for special education placement actually know very little about tests and psychological evaluation.

HISTORY OF THE TESTING MOVEMENT

There were very few developments in testing prior to 1879 when a research laboratory was established in Leipzig by Wilhelm Wundt (1832-1920) and became the birthplace of psychological measurement as a scientific field of endeavor.

Wundt and his colleagues laid the groundwork over a hundred years ago in formulating theories of learning which apply to nearly all of the human species. These theories or "laws" are still being debated and expanded today. Recently this area has come under considerable speculation and investigation concerning its potential for early stimulation of high risk children. According to Gearheart and Willenberg "The past centennial constitutes some banner years in developing a greater understanding of how and why humans develop, learn, and behave as they do—and the implications of such understandings for educators" (1980, p. 5).

An American, James M. Cattell (1860-1944), studied with Wundt at Leipzig and appears to be the first person to use the term "mental test." Cattell and his associates perceived that the measuring of individual differences could have far reaching effects in the schools and also in industry. Cattell and others had an overwhelming goal of finding a way to assess general intelligence.

Sir Francis Galton (1822-1911) played a very important role in the development of the testing movement. He originated two statistical concepts which caused the psychometric field to flourish. These two concepts were regression to the mean and correlation. These concepts according to Sattler (1982, p. 30) "allowed for the study of intelligence over time, and for the study of the relationship of intelligence test scores between parent and child (as well as other relationships)."

Galton established a psychometric laboratory in 1884. This laboratory was first established at the International Health Exhibition but was later reestablished at University College, London. Sir Francis Galton is regarded by many to be the true father of the testing movement.

In France Alfred Binet (1857-1911), Victor Henri (1872-1940), and Theodore Simon (1873-1961) developed methods for the study of a variety of mental functions. These investigators discovered the key to the measurement of intelligence and their work was culminated in the publication of the 1905 Binet-Simon Scale. Although the scale was not novel because many of the items had been published in various papers, it can still be considered the first modern intelligence test.

Swanson and Watson (1982, p. 9) stated that the Binet-Simon Test had several unique characteristics:

(1) questions were arranged in a hierarchy of difficulty, (2) levels were established for different ages (establishment of mental age), (3) a quantitative scoring system was applied, and (4) specific instructions for administration were built into the test.

The testing movement began to flourish in the United States after the introduction of the Binet-Simon Scale. H.H. Goddard translated the Binet-Simon Scale for use in the United States in 1908. Lewis Terman standardized the Binet-Simon Scale in 1916 and with Maud Merrill revised them in 1937 and 1960.

Terman in the 1916 translation increased the length of the test by adding several new scales. Terman's revision was called the Stanford-Binet and the original tests were aligned to age levels according to the new norms and the concept of the intelligence quotient was added to the mental age (Swanson and Watson, 1982).

Charles E. Spearman (1863-1945) was an early proponent of a factor analytic approach to intelligence. In 1927 Spearman proposed a two factor theory of intelligence which stated that a general factor (g) plus one specific factor per test accounts for one's performance on an intelligence test. To Spearman the g factor was thought of as a general mental energy with complicated mental activities having the highest amount of g. This factor involves the operation of a deductive nature and is linked with a skill. It is also linked with speed, intensity, and extensity of an individual's intellectual output. The cognitive activities associated with g as expressed by Sattler (1982, p. 38):

are eduction of relations (determining the relationship between two or more ideas) and eduction of correlates (finding a second idea associated with a previously stated one). Any intellectual activity involves both a general factor, which it shares with all other intellectual activities, and a specific factor, which it shares with none.

Guilford (1967) conducted some ambitious research relating to intelligence and in the measure of human attributes. Guilford's model (Figure 1.1) includes a cross-classification of attributes with intersecting categories instead of discrete attributes within categories. His model also provides three major categories with subclasses in each. Guilford's theoretical model contains five subclasses of operations, four classes of content and six subclass products for a total of 120 different abilities. According to Swanson and Watson (1983, p. 12) "an intellectual factor in assessing children can result when any one of the five operations combines with any one of the six products and any one of the four contents."

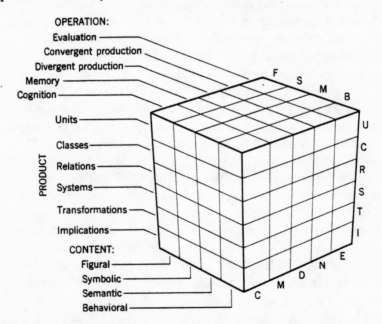

Figure 1-1. Guilford's structure of the intellect model by three dimensions. (From Guilford, P. *The nature of human intelligence.* New York: McGraw-Hill, 1967, p. 63). Reprinted with permission of publisher.

Vernon (1965) notes that many of Guilford's factors of intellect do not show any external validity which could not be accounted for by their general or group values. Eysenck (1967) criticized Guilford's model because it did not reproduce the very essential hierarchical nature of intelligence test data.

A proposal has been made by Arthur Jenson (1970, 1980) that mental abilities fall into two major classes: Level I which is associative and Level II which is cognitive. Rote learning is involved in the associative ability as well as short term memory. This is measured by tasks which involve digit span memory, free recall, serial learning and paired-associate learning. In cognitive ability we find reasoning and problem solving and we can measure these by the tests of general intelligence. Most individual general intelligence tests have tasks which involve reasoning, problem solving, use of concepts, verbal and figural analogies, number series and possibly progressive matrices. Most intelligence tests are likely to measure both of Jensen's levels.

The distinction between level I and II involves a difference in the complexity of the transformation and mental manipulations that occur between the presentation of a given mental task and the response (Sattler, 1982).

David Wechsler (1896-1981) found himself during World War I involved in the large scale intelligence testing program conducted by the army. This work so impressed Private Wechsler that he spent the rest of his life engaged in discovering better measurements of intelligence and his work led to major contributions in both theory and practice.

Wechsler received a Ph.D. from Columbia University in 1925 and by 1932 had become chief psychologist at Bellevue Psychiatric Hospital.

Starting in 1934 and continuing to his death he was instrumental in developing intelligence scales which are internationally known: the Wechsler-Bellevue I published in 1939, the Wechsler-Bellevue II or Army Wechsler (1942), the Wechsler Intelligence Scale for Children (1949), the Wechsler Adult Intelligence Scale (1955), the Wechsler Preschool and Primary Scale of Intelligence (1967), the Revision of the Wechsler Intelligence Scale for Children (1974) and the Revision of the Wechsler Adult Intelligence Scale (1981).

DIFFERENCES BETWEEN INTELLIGENCE TESTS AND ACHIEVEMENT TESTS

Intelligence tests and achievement tests have likenesses and differences. Humphreys (1971) notes that both types of tests sample aptitude, learning, and achievement and they both sample responses in the child's repertoire at the testing session. The two types of tests also differ in a number of ways. Intelligence tests sample a much wider range of experiences than do achievement tests. Achievement tests are not as valid for measuring learning potential as are intelligence tests. A score on a mathematical subtest of an achievement test, for example, is heavily dependent on formal learning experiences acquired in school. Intelligence tests measure less formal achievement than achievement tests and they also measure the ability to apply information in new ways. Achievement tests stress mastery of factual information such as reading, math, English usage, etc.

PLACEMENT TESTS

These tests notes Gearheart and Willenberg (1980) are tests used to determine whether a given student is ready to move into a new unit or a new area of study. These tests are referred to as readiness tests and they might be standardized or teacher-made, but, regardless, the purpose is to determine the degree of readiness or the level at which a child is working. Placement tests are also given to determine if a child is eligible for a special education program. After all requirements for special education have been met, there may be a need for additional assessment to determine which type of program components the child should need. This is called assessment testing.

DIAGNOSTIC TESTS

In diagnostic testing we evaluate in order to determine specific learning disabilities and provide guidance for individual program planning. In the special education placement process some diagnostic testing is performed but it is essential that diagnostic testing take place at periodic intervals during the student's program. Program planning should revolve around diagnostic testing and program modifications should come about only after diagnostic testing.

FORMAL, STANDARDIZED TESTS

It should be pointed out that formal standardized tests of academic achievement, listening vocabulary, intelligence tests, behavior rating scales, etc. are more important to administrators than to teachers. For example, the formal academic achievement tests enable administrators and subject matter specialists who are responsible for the overall curriculum to judge how students compare in a given district, area, state or the nation. The tests which are more important for classroom use though are teacher made tests.

INFORMAL TESTING

To describe an individual performance in basic skill areas, the testing of choice is that developed by the teacher using classroom materials. Informal testing should examine behaviors which the teacher wants the student to demonstrate in daily work; therefore the teacher should select the test items from texts the student uses in the classroom. In informal testing the teacher must be able to recognize a random error as opposed to a consistent skill deficit. Because the teacher has the opportunity to base informal testing on the student's work he/she is not likely to mistake a random mistake as a skill deficit. Only those skills which appear to be in deficit need to be tested. The cumulative record will yield the strengths of students in subject matter areas.

Table 1.1

COMPARISON OF NORM-REFERENCED TESTS
AND CRITERION-REFERENCED TESTS

Advantages

Norm-Referenced Tests	*Criterion-Referenced Tests*
1. Emphasizes competition with self; de-emphasizes competition with others.	1. Reference points are fixed at specified, cut-off points and do not depend on a reference group.
2. Helps to determine if a student is achieving up to expectations.	2. Evaluates individual performances in relation to a fixed standard; student competing against self.
3. Evaluates individual performance in comparison to a group of persons; student competing against others.	3. Is content-specific.
4. Designed to maximize variability and produce scores that are normally distributed.	4. Tests are directly referenced to the objectives of instruction.
	5. Identifies those segments of the spectrum of objectives the individual has mastered.

Disadvantages

Norm-Referenced Tests	*Criterion-Referenced Tests*
1. Is vague in relation to the specific instructional content.	1. Many teachers not well equipped to construct such tests.
2. Tests have a low degree of overlap with actual objectives of instruction.	2. Standards may tend to be arbitrary.
3. Generally a poor aid in planning instruction.	3. Cannot measure achievement gains as compared to other children.
4. Tests not sensitive to the effects of instruction.	4. Of little value in identifying the special needs student.

Summative evaluation occurs at the end of six weeks or nine weeks and again at the end of the course. This evaluation is typically used to assign grades and is accomplished by criterion-referenced tests as opposed to norm referenced tests.

A norm-referenced test provides a comparison with some norm group. In other words it is a test in which the test results or scores are related to scores for a specific group of students. Often this type of testing leads to grade equivalents, mental age estimates, and so forth.

A criterion-referenced test is one in which the measure of a student's mastery of particular skills in terms of absolute mastery is measured. In this type of testing we get answers to specific questions such as "Does Susie spell the word *cat* correctly?" Criterion-referenced tests treat the pupil as an individual instead of providing numerical indexes of performance typically expected of others.

To end this chapter, the author would like to call attention to Table 1.1 which compares norm-referenced and criterion-referenced tests.

BIBLIOGRAPHY

Bersoff, D.N.: Silk purses into sow's ears: The decline of psychological testing and a suggestion for its redemption. *American Psychologist, 28*:892-899, 1973.

Cleveland, S.: Reflections on the rise and fall of psycho-diagnosis. *Professional Psychology, 7*:301-318, 1976.

Crawford, C.: George Washington, Abraham Lincoln and Arthur Jenson: Are they compatible? *American Psychologist, 34*:664-672, 1979.

Eysenck, H.J.: Intelligence assessment: A theoretical and experimental approach. *British Journal of Educational Psychology, 37*:81-98, 1967.

Gearheart, Bill R. and Willenberg, Ernest P.: *Application of pupil assessment information*, 3rd ed. Denver, Love Publishing Co., 1980.

Guilford, P.: *The nature of human intelligence*. New York, McGraw-Hill, 1967.

Humphreys, L.G.: Theory of intelligence. In R. Cancro (Ed.): *Intelligence: Genetic and Environmental Influences*. New York, Grune and Stratton, 1971.

Sattler, Jerome M.: *Assessment of Children's Intelligence and Special Abilities*, 2nd ed. Boston, Allyn and Bacon, 1982.

Scott, M.: Ecological theory and methods for research in special education. *Journal of Special Education, 14*:279-294, 1980.

Smith, C., and Knoff, H.: School psychology and special education students' placement decisions: IQ still tips the scale. *Journal of Special Education, 15*:55-64, 1981.

Swanson, H. Lee and Watson, Billy L.: *Educational and Psychological Assessment of Exceptional Children: Theories, Strategies, and Applications*. St. Louis, Mosby, 1982.

Vernon, P.E.: Ability factors and environmental influences. *American Psychologist, 20*:723-733, 1965.

CHAPTER 2

PURPOSES OF AND ASSUMPTIONS IN ASSESSMENT

THE American Psychological Association (APA), the American Educational Research Association (AERA), and the National Council on Measurement in Education (NCME) all agree that a test "may be thought of as a set of tasks or questions intended to elicit particular types of behaviors when presented under standardized conditions and to yield scores that have desirable psychometric properties" (1974, p. 2). When we test students, they are exposed to a particular set of questions and a score is obtained. Naturally, that score is the end product of the testing.

PURPOSES OF ASSESSMENT

Tests are administered to children in an educational setting for many reasons. The professionals who administer psychological and educational tests do so to better help in making decisions that will aid the student in his educational development.

Salvia and Ysseldyke (1978) tell us that there are at least five specific reasons for giving tests to students; screening, placement, program planning, program evaluation, and assessment of the student's progress.

A small portion of this chapter is adapted from the following work: Love, Harold D.: *Teaching Mildly Handicapped Children — Methods and Materials*, Charles C Thomas, Publisher, 1984.

IDENTIFICATION

How and when are the exceptional children identified? Who makes decisions on the instructional programs needed? Are the placement decisions temporary or permanent? These are some questions raised by educators and administrators when beginning to learn about educational programming for exceptional children and youth.

Before Public Law 94-142 became a reality, the typical approach to identifying the exceptional child was to rely on referrals or to conduct screening programs. Today, though, states are required by federal law to identify and report the number of handicapped children between the ages of three and twenty-one. One new way of identification has resulted in Child Find activities. Meyen and Lehr (1982, p. 66) make the following comments about Child Find:

> A recently developed approach, Child Find, involves public awareness activities and mass campaigns aimed at identifying those ages 0-21 with special needs. News media, posters, handbills, mail-out questionnaires, telephone surveys, referrals, and other techniques have elicited broad public involvement. Assistance is sought from service clubs, churches, physicians, public agencies, day care facilities, Chambers of Commerce, and other entities such as private nurseries. The intent is to build a registry of children and youth thought to have special needs . . .

> Child Find activities are more than public announcements and surveys, though. Each educational agency has written procedures describing its Child Find activities and maintains basic data on the children identified. This information generally includes the child's name and address, how the child was identified, date of identification, and services needed or being provided.

Child Find activities to date have been fairly successful. The one area where the program has been especially successful is in identifying young handicapped children.

Screening

This is a systematic approach to identifying students who may need special education services. Parental permission should be obtained before any screening takes place. The regular classroom teacher should not over-refer because diagnostic testing of some exceptional or handicapping conditions require considerable time and skill on the part of the specialist administering the tests. Sometimes more than one specialist will be involved.

The Referral

The referral process by the regular class teacher is a very simple process. It is intended to provide a mechanism which will bring suspected handicapping conditions in students to the attention of appropriate professionals without much delay. Referral forms are typically across a district, but occasionally you find them state wide. Table 2.1 is a referral form used in North Carolina and is one that the author likes because it incorporates the eight problem areas mentioned in P.L. 94-142. The teacher fills out this form and mentions the behavior of the child which makes him/her think than an exceptionality may be present.

Referrals may arise from sources other than regular classroom teachers, of course. School personnel such as counselors, principals, and school nurses sometimes initiate referrals, as do community sources such as physicians, private schools, clergymen and women, departments of public health and social agencies. In many cases the parents contact the school personnel and ask for an evaluation.

The student's parents should be helped to understand the referral process and why their child is being referred. The parent's permission is required before an actual evaluation can take place. Later, if the child is placed in special education the parents will then be involved in developing the IEP. They also have information that can be of value and can allow insight into any cultural differences that may be contributing to the child's ability.

The child can be evaluated after the parents give permission. The information on the referral form is reviewed by an appropriate specialist — psychologist, speech clinician, school nurse, or other expert as the need suggests.

Table 2.1

REFERRAL FORM

Name _____ Birthdate _____ Age _____

School _____ Grade _____ Sex _____

Parents/Guardians _____

Address _____ Phone _____

Referred By _____ Position _____

PROBLEM AREAS

Acculturation & Language _____

Health (Medical) _____

_____

Hearing _____

_____

Vision _____

_____

Speech _____

_____

Perceptual-Motor Performance _____

_____

Academic Achievement & Intelligence _____

_____

Social-Emotional Behavior _____

_____

Parental Involvement _____

_____

Other Comments:

INAPPROPRIATE OR INCORRECT
CLASSIFICATION OR LABELING

After the child has been referred for testing, we assume that the testing will be fair for each child tested and placed in special services. This, of course, has not always been the case as evidenced by a case known as *Larry P. v. Riles* filed in California November 18, 1971 on behalf of specific plaintiffs who were Black children in that state wrongly placed in special classes for the educable mentally retarded. According to Gearheart (1980, p. 20) the:

> plaintiffs alleged that they (and the class they represented) had been wrongly placed in classes for the mentally retarded as a result of inappropriate testing procedures, which ignored their unique home experiences and failed to recognize their unfamiliarity with White, middle class culture. The complaint also alleged that such a placement procedure violated the Civil Rights Act and the right to equal protection as guaranteed by the California Constitution and the Fourteenth Amendment of the U.S. Constitution, which prohibits discrimination based on race or color.

In most cases which have come before the judiciary the parties involved have signed consent agreements which attempted to rectify unfair procedures which involved ethnic minorities. Also, PL 94-142 has provisions which attempt to protect the rights of ethnic minority children. Sattler (1982, pp. 525-526) notes that although provisions have been made to protect the rights of ethnic minority children that in the case of *Larry P. Riles*:

> a federal court ordered the State of California to cease to use intelligence tests for the assessment of Black children for placement in educable mentally retarded classes. The court did not interpret the provisions of PL 94-142 to mean that intelligence tests must be used in conjunction with other measures to arrive at the diagnosis of mental retardation. In contrast, a federal court in Illinois ruled in the *Parents in Action on Special Education v. Joseph P. Hannon* case that intelligence tests are not culturally biased against Black children.

Further, this court stipulated that when used with other criteria in the assessment process, intelligence tests comply with federal guidelines concerning the use of nondiscriminatory procedures. The issues raised by minorities, as we have seen, are complex, and simple and clear-cut answers are not always available.

In the case of *Diana v. State Board of Education* also filed in California it was alleged that the use of biased tests were used to place Mexican-American and Chinese children in classes for the educable mentally retarded. In this case the school system agreed that linguistically different children would be tested both in their primary language and in English, that primarily nonverbal tests would be used for the assessment of these children's cognitive skills, and that an interpreter would be used when a bilingual examiner is not available.

OTHER ASSUMPTIONS

One assumption we make, according to Newland (1971), is that the person giving the test is skilled. We assume that the evaluator has adequate training for the purpose of testing. We also assume that the testor knows how to establish rapport with children and we further assume that the testor knows how to administer the tests correctly. We also assume that the person who administers the tests knows how to properly score them. Finally, we assume that the testor can accurately interpret the results.

Obviously, it is very important that the person who administers the test be skilled and qualified educationally as well. It is noted by Salvia and Ysseldyke (1978, p. 17) that:

Too often, unfortunately, we hear of people with no training in individual intelligence testing who nonetheless administer individual intelligence tests; or we see people with no formal training in personality test administration or interpretation giving personality tests. Such tests may *look* easy enough to give; however, the correct administration, scoring, and interpretation are complex.

We assume that the recommendations in psychological reports will be followed by school administrators, special educators, regular class teachers, etc. The following case clearly illustrates what can happen when recommendations in psychological write-ups are not followed.

DANIEL HOFFMAN v. THE BOARD OF EDUCATION OF THE CITY OF NEW YORK*

When Daniel was 5 years, 9 months old he scored an I.Q. of 74 on the Stanford-Binet and was placed in a class for the educable mentally retarded. The report was written in 1957 and the key sentence in the report follows: "Also, his intelligence should be reevaluated within a two year period so that a more accurate estimation of his abilities can be made." Daniel entered special education classes in 1957 and remained in classes for the educable mentally retarded for the rest of his school years.

At the age of 17 years Daniel was placed in a shop training school for retarded youths. After he had spent a few months in the program the Wechsler Adult Intelligence Scale (WAIS) was administered to Daniel. He had a Verbal I.Q. of 85, a Performance I.Q. of 107 and a Full Scale I.Q. of 94. The average range of intelligence is from 90-109; therefore, Daniel fell into the average range. Because he was not retarded, Daniel was not allowed to remain at the Occupational Training Center.

At the age of 21 years, after training from Vocational Rehabilitation, Daniel tried to work as a messenger but did not like the job.

At the age of 26 years Daniel brought suit against the New York City Board of Education for damages for being placed in a special class for educable mentally retarded children. He also sued because he had not had adequate speech therapy, his only real handicap, since he was not retarded.

During the trial it was discovered that Daniel's first psychologist did not interview his mother, did not discuss the results of the testing with her and did not take a social history. If the psychologist had taken a social history he would have known that Daniel had been tested ten months earlier at the National Hospital for Speech Disorders and had scored an I.Q. of 90 on the Merrill-Palmer Scale of Mental Tests.

Daniel's case was originally heard by a jury and he was awarded damages of $750,000. This decision was appealed to the Appellate Division of the New York State Supreme Court which affirmed the jury verdict but lowered the damages to $500,000. On December 17, 1979 the

---

*Adapted from *Assessment of Children's Intelligence and Special Abilities* by Sattler, Jerome M., Allyn and Bacon, Inc., 1982.

New York State Appeals Court overturned the Appellate Court's decision and found that the court system is not the proper arena for testing the validity of educational policy making and decisions.

No matter the final outcome of Daniel's case against the Board of Education of New York City, we can see that this case is important to the practice of school and clinical psychology. The fact that the recommendations in a psychological write-up were not followed had a dramatic impact on a man's life. Also, it is the first case in which the courts carefully examined a psychological report and placement in special education.

The case of *Daniel Hoffman v. Board of Education of the city of New York* brings to light many invalid assumptions held by teachers and other professionals who work with children. Daniel was tested with three different intelligence tests and, of course, the examiners got three different scores. People should realize that the standardization procedures of the three tests are different and this difference is reflected in the scores made by Daniel. Teachers should not assume that I.Q.s are static because they are not. We do know that after the age of 6 years, I.Q.s are fairly static, but certainly they do change.

TESTING MINORITY CHILDREN

We assume that when we test children we do not discriminate against a large segment of the population known as *ethnic minority group children*. These children come from certain groups which include Blacks, Mexican-Americans, American Indians, Puerto Ricans, and Asian Americans. These groups are subcultures which do not always conform to the patterns of the majority group. Barnes (1971) notes that certain unstandard groups may be both healthy and justified, because life conditions of these groups differ markedly from those of the dominant culture. Actually, this author believes that the extent to which a group is handicapped in testing or anything else lies in the eyes of the beholder.

The Education Department's Office for Civil Rights (OCR) found that Black children represented thirty-eight percent of all elementary and secondary students. This has caused a controversy because of the use of I.Q. tests which civil rights groups have termed racially biased. However, a panel convened by the National Academy of Sciences found that racial imbalance in special education programs does not pose a major problem unless the disproportion results from improper assessment procedures and inadequate instructional practices.

In its review of the OCR surveys and other studies the panel convened by the National Academy of Sciences found insufficient evidence to support charges that I.Q. tests discriminate against minority group children and questioned the wisdom of abandoning I.Q. tests and EMR classes.

In the panel's three year study report entitled "Placing Children in Special Education: A Study for Equity," it recommended improvement of current assessment procedures and educational services rather than remedies that would directly eliminate disproportion in placement rates.

Wayne H. Holtzman of the Hogg Foundation for Mental Health at the University of Texas, who chaired the fifteen member panel, has suggested that instead of relying on I.Q. tests solely, school districts should use intelligence tests in combination with several other instruments to determine appropriate placement and instruction.

Garth (1928) reported the results of testing 1,004 Mexican-American children when he found significantly lower scores than the standardization sample. He did not cite language as a major contributing factor to the lower scores. However, Garth, Elson, and Morton (1936) cited language as a major factor when Mexican-American children were tested with verbal tests of intelligence.

Mitchell (1937) administered a Spanish translation of the Otis Group intelligence Scale to Mexican-American children and followed with the English version. He found that the subjects scored significantly higher in the Spanish version than in the English version (Spanish MA 13.2, English MA 7.6). Mahakian (1939) used the same tests and had very similar results. Both authors concluded the same thing — intelligence tests administered in English to Spanish speaking children are not valid. In a later study, Keston and Jimenez (1954) found that Mexican-American children scored higher on the Spanish version of the WISC and Binet than on the English version.

At the present time, only New Mexico has not accepted Public Law 94-142 and funding that comes with it. A class action case was filed in 1975, *New Mexico Association for Retarded Chidren et al v. New Mexico State Board of Education.* Swanson and Watson (1982) state that the defendants were charged with discrimination in the following areas:

1. Inadequate and inappropriate level of supportive services.
2. Inadequate number of diagnosticians resulting in delays in the evaluation process and consequent services.
3. Failure to establish and enforce appropriate standards.
4. Failure to properly budget funds.
5. Failure to provide qualified personnel to adequately serve plaintiffs.

The judge ruled in favor of the plaintiffs with a plan being submitted for the purpose of remediating all discriminatory practices. The case is currently under appeal. A more recent case brought before the U.S. District Court of New Mexico is *Rodney Schells v Albuquerque Public School District* (1979). This class-action suit was filed in behalf of low-income minority Albuquerque Public School students purportedly misclassified as educable mentally retarded based on discriminatory intelligence tests and evaluation procedures (Swanson and Watson, 1982, p. 379).

Valentine (1971) notes that Black Americans are bicultural and bidialectal, and far from being either deficient or merely different in culture. They often possess a richer repertoire of life styles than middle class Whites. In discussing why there is a difference in Afro-American behavior, Valentine (1971, p. 143) argued for a bicultural model. Biculturation is the:

key concept for making sense out of ethnicity and related matters: the collective behavior and social life of the Black community is bicultural in the sense that each Afro-American ethnic segment draws upon both a distinctive repertoire of standardized Afro-American group behavior and, simultaneously, patterns derived from the mainstream cultural system of Euro-American derivation.

The cultural diversity which exists within the Black community makes any generalizations about Black children suspect. However, the pattern of race relations in our country is likely to have had similar effects on Black children, regardless of their particular individual cultural style (Sattler, 1982).

As far as testing is concerned, differences in dialect have been cited as a potential source of difficulty between White examiners and Black children. There is an argument that Black children do not understand White examiners; therefore, they make lower I.Q. scores. Quay (1972, 1974), however, reported that Black children did not make higher scores when the Stanford-Binet was administered by a Black examiner in Black dialect instead of Standard English. Sattler (1982) states that "there is increasing evidence that Black children are bidialectal, in that they have the ability to comprehend equally well Black dialect and standard English."

Indians are an impoverished group in our society and at the present time there are about 1.4 million American Indians which constitutes less than one percent of the U.S. population.

The outlook for Indian children in our schools is not very good and work is quite limited for Indian children and youth. The drop out rate in school for the Indian children is double that of the national average. Indian children face a bleak future as evidenced by the quotation below by Farris and Farris (1976, p. 386):

> The Indian child can look forward to little more than a fifth-grade education; he and 95 percent of his classmates will probably drop out before high school. His self-image reflects this if, indeed, it is not the cause of his failure. More than any group, Indian children believe themselves to be of below-average intelligence. Boarding schools and long separations from family are commonplace. It is not unheard of for an Indian child in Alaska to be sent to a school run by the Bureau of Indian Affairs in Oklahoma. In 1973 there were over 33,000 children living away from their homes and families. And these schools, where his teachers are usually non-

Indian, will further erode his self-esteem.

Garth (1933) in one of the earlier studies comparing different minority ethnic groups in intelligence between five "blood groups of White, Indian and Mexican children" had this to say:

> If these groups may be taken as representative of their racial stocks, the results indicate differences between their racial stocks in intelligence as here measured, one is inclined to believe that differences in mental attitude toward the White man's way of thinking and living are here made apparent (p. 401).

In an earlier work Yerkes (1923, p. 80) commented on the interpretation of the I.Q. score and warned:

> Never should such a diagnosis be made on the IQ alone . . . We must inquire further into the subject's economic history. What is his occupation; his pay? We must learn what we can about his immediate family. What is the economic status or occupation of his parents? When . . . this information has been collected . . . the psychologist may be of great value in getting the subject into the most suitable place in society.

There are studies which indicate that Indian children may obtain performance I.Q.s 25-30 points higher than their verbal I.Q. scores. According to Krywaniuk and Das (1976), this pattern of achievement may be a reflection of a visual style of learning and limited ability with English usage.

Mickelson and Galloway (1973) found that Indian children begin school with less developed verbal concept ability as measured by the Boehm Test of Basic Concepts. This would indicate that these children need remedial English programs and programs to help them develop better verbal concepts.

The author would be remiss if he did not mention Puerto Rican children in the eastern U.S. and Cuban children living in Florida. More than one million Cubans live in Florida and more than two million Puerto Ricans live in the United States with sixty percent of them living in New York City. Both groups speak Spanish and they are economically deprived groups, making meager incomes with unemployment running high and the educational level being low.

There have been several intelligence tests translated into Spanish with Sheldon (1924) being the first to use Spanish-speaking teachers for the administration of group tests. Paschal and Sullivan (1925) were the first to translate the Stanford-Binet into Spanish and Mitchell (1937) was the first person to translate the Otis Group Intelligence Test into Spanish. Mitchell (1937) found that Spanish speaking children did significantly better on his version and Mahakian (1939) had similar results.

The WISC was translated into the Spanish of Puerto Rico (1949) and the WAIS was translated by Green (1964). It is interesting to note that studies have shown that Mexican-American children consistently score lower on the Spanish version than on the English version. There have been many studies which criticized the translations (Quay, 1971; Samuda, 1975; and Mercer, 1979).

Researchers have found the inability to derive the equivalence in vocabulary of the two languages. Other problems arise when one thinks of the numerous words for which there are no equivalents in other languages.

Another error which occurs, according to Swanson and Watson (1982), is when errors occur:

> on tests in which items become progressively more difficult, such as the WISC-R and the Peabody Picture Vocabulary Test. A translated word may have a different level of difficulty in other languages and will, therefore, invalidate the procedures for obtaining the basals and ceilings for these instruments. Once translated, items must be rearranged into order of difficulty. One must not at any time assume that, once translated, the test or any part of the test has the same degree of difficulty or validity (pp. 381-82).

This author agrees with a summary statement made by Sattler (1982, pp. 365-66) in Chapter Nineteen of his book about the assessment of children's intelligence and special abilities:

> In summary, we have seen that intelligence tests (and other ability tests) measure the abilities that they were designed to measure with reasonable accuracy for ethnic minority chil-

dren and for children from the dominant culture as well. Tests have the potential to do much good in our society. Tests assess a child's current intellectual functioning irrespective of race or social status. Thus, the consequences of not testing might be to increase bias and discrimination.

SUMMARY

We often make assumptions concerning the tests which we administer and most of the assumptions are correct; however, some are not. We assume that the standardization procedure was adequate and that the tests are valid and reliable. However, until we read the manual which accompanies the tests, we don't know if these assumptions are correct. We also assume that the person giving the test is skilled and that he has adequate training for the purpose of administering the tests. Usually we are right but on some occasions we find people who have the training but still don't have the knowledge.

We further assume that our tests don't discriminate against minorities. The research seems to back this assumption in spite of what many critics say. Green (1978, p. 669) argues that "the tests are not bigoted villains but color blind measuring instruments that have demonstrated a social problem to be solved." The American Psychological Association's Board of Scientific Affairs (1975, p. 18) stressed that "Diagnosis, prognosis, prescription, and measurement of outcomes are as important in education as in medicine."

BIBLIOGRAPHY

American Psychological Association, American Educational Research Association, and National Council on Measurement in Education: Standards for Educational and Psychological Tests. Washington, D.C., American Psychological Association, 1974.

Barnes, E.C.: The utilization of behavioral and social sciences in minority group education: Some critical implications. In W.R. Rhine (Chair), *Ethnic minority issues on the utilization of behavioral and social science in a pluralistic society*. Symposium presented at the meeting of the American Psychological Association, Washington, D.C., Sept. 1971.

Cleary, T.A., Humphrey, L.G., Kendrick, S.A., and Wesman, A.: Educational uses of tests with disadvantaged students. *American Psychologist, 30*:15-41, 1975.

Farris, C.E. and Farris, L.S.: Indian children: The struggle for survival. *Social Work, 21*:386-389, 1976.

Garth, T.R.: The intelligence and achievement of mixed blood Indians. *Journal of Social Psychology, 4*:234-237, 1933.

Gearheart, Bill R. and Willenberg, Ernest P.: *Application of pupil assessment information*, 3rd ed. Denver, Love Publishing Co., 1980.

Green, B.F., Jr.: In defense of measurement. *American Psychologist, 33*:664-670, 1978.

Green, R.F.: Desarollo y estandarización de una escala individual de inteligencia para adultos en español (The development and standardization of an individual intelligence scale for adults in Spanish). *Revista Mexicana de Psicolgia, 1*:231-244, 1964.

Krywaniuk, L.W. and Das, J.P.: Cognitive strategies in native children: Analysis and intervention. *Alberta Journal of Educational Research, 22*:271-280, 1976.

Mahakian, C.: Measuring the intelligence and reading capacity of Spanish-speaking children. *Elementary School Journal, 39*:760-768, 1939.

Mercer, J.R.: *SOMPA Technical Manual*. New York, Psychological Corporation, 1979.

Meyen, Edward L. and Lehr, Donna.: *Exceptional Children in Today's Schools: An alternative resource book*. Denver, Love Publishing Co., 1982.

Mickelson, N.I. and Galloway, C.G.: Verbal concepts of Indian and nonIndian school beginners. *Journal of Education Research, 67*:55-56, 1973.

Mitchell, A.J.: The effect of bilingualism on the measurement of intelligence. *Elementary School Journal, 38*:29-37, 1937.

Newland, T.E.: Assumptions underlying psychological testing. *Journal of School Psychology, 11*:316-322, 1973.

Paschal, F.C. and Sullivan, L.R.: Racial differences in the mental and psychological development of Mexican children. *Comparative Psychology Monographs, 3*:(2), 1925.

Quay, L.: Language, dialect, reinforcement and the intelligence test performance of Negro children. *Child Development, 42*:5-15, 1971.

Quay, L.C.: Language, dialect, age and intelligence-test performance in disadvantaged Black children. *Child Development, 45*:463-468, 1974.

Quay, L.C.: Negro dialect and Binet performance in severely disadvantaged Black four-year-olds. *Child Development, 43*:245-250, 1972.

Salvia, John and Ysseldyke, James E.: *Assessment in Special and Remedial Education*. Dallas, Houghton-Mifflin, 1978.

Samuda, R.S.: *Psychological testing of American minorities: Issues and consequences*. New York, Dodd, Mead, 1975.

Sattler, Jerome M.: *Assessment of Children's Intelligence and Special Abilities*, 2nd ed. Boston, Allyn and Bacon, 1982.

Sheldon, W.H.: The intelligence of Mexican children. *School and Society, 19*:129-142, 1924.

Swanson, H. Lee and Watson, Billy L.: *Educational and Psychological Assessment of Exceptional Children: Theories, strategies, and applications.* St. Louis, Mosby, 1982.

Valentine, C.A.: Deficit, difference, and bicultural models of Afro-American behavior. *Harvard Educational Review, 41*:137-157, 1971.

Yerkes, R.M. and Foster, J.C.: *A point scale for measuring mental ability.* Baltimore, Warwick and York, 1923.

CHAPTER 3

TERMS, CONCEPTS AND GLOSSARY

THERE are certain terms and concepts which are routinely discussed in the total evaluative procedure. The author realizes that many readers are already familiar with many of the terms and concepts necessary to describe and discuss various evaluative tools used in education and psychology. However, for those who are not familiar, a brief overview, including concise definitions is presented in this chapter.

Measures of Central Tendency

These are the mean, median and mode. They are often used in comparing tests and students.

Mean. The average score. This measure is found by adding all scores and dividing the sum by the total number of individual scores.

Median. The "middle-most" score. One-half of all scores are found above this score and one-half are found below this score. This measure is found by listing all scores from greatest to least, or from least to greatest, counting them, dividing the total number of scores by 2, and counting down to that number. If it is between two numbers, take their mean.

Mode. The most frequently occurring score. This is found by recording all scores and finding the one that occurs more than any other score. The mode (Mo) is seldom used, but may be of interest historically. In the distribution 12, 16, 10, 9, 9, 8, 7, the mode is 9.

Measures of Variability

It is valuable to know how test scores are distributed around the central measure. It is very possible to have two or three sets of scores with the same mean but with a different spread of scores. It is quite possible that this spread of scores may be the most important characteristic of the distribution. Probably the simplest measure of variability is the *range*. The *range*, simply stated, is the numerical difference between the high and low scores. If the lowest scores in the class is 10 and the highest is 25, the range is 15.

Another measure of variability is the *semi-interquartile range*. The range is very sensitive to the presence of a small number of scores at either the low or high extremes of the distribution, therefore, the *semi-interquartile range* may be more valuable. In simple language it is one-half the range of the middle fifty percent of the scores. We find the point below which seventy-five percent of the scores lie. This is Q_3 or the third quartile. Next we find the point below which twenty-five percent of the scores lie. This is Q_1 or the first quartile. Next, we subtract the first quartile from the third quartile and divide by two.

Another measure of variability is the *standard deviation* (SD). The SD of a set of scores is a statistic which expresses the variability of the scores. If most of the scores cluster at or near the mean (for example 4, 5, 6), then the SD will be small. However, if there is a great deal of variability in the scores (for example 1, 30, 90), the SD will be large. The SD may be calculated for any set of scores by using the following formula.

$$SD = \sqrt{\frac{\Sigma x^2 - \dfrac{(\Sigma x)^2}{N}}{N-1}}$$

The Normal Curve

The normal (bell) curve is a statistical term which refers to the distribution of general characteristics of various types of data. The characteristics of sets of physical properties found in an average population often fall into a symmetrical distribution. this distribution is known as a normal curve.

The normal curve can be used to show the distribution and frequency of intelligence quotients found in an average or normal population.

The full or high part of the curve occurs around 100 and represents the area into which the largest percentages of I.Q.'s occur. The ends of the curve taper sharply to represent the increasingly smaller groups of higher than average and lower than average I.Q.'s found in a normal population.

The following table shows the percentages of the population expected to fall into each I.Q. classification based on a normal curve.

Intelligence Classification

Classification	Percent
130 and above	2.2
120-129	6.7
110-119	16.1
90-109	50.0
80-89	16.1
70-79	6.7
69 and below	2.2

This information can also be charted as follows:

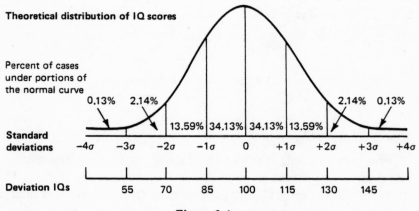

Figure 3.1.

Percentile Rank

Percentile rank permits us to determine an individual's position relative to the standardization sample. A percentile score is a point in the distribution at or below which a given percentage of individuals fall. If sixty-five percent of the cases fall below a given score, then that score is at the sixty-fifth percentiles.

A person who obtains a percentile rank of thirty on an intelligence test has scored as well or better than thirty percent of the individuals in the norm sample.

Percentile rank refers to where the score you make on a test is in relation to other scores (usually obtained by a control group, or sample group) on the same test. In theory, if one hundred people were given a test they would be ranked from 1 to 100 regardless of the test scores (either the high or low score). Percentile rank should not be confused with percentage. A percentile rank of seventy means you scored as well as or better than seventy percent of the people in the sample that took the same test. It may or may not mean you made seventy percent on the test.

Deciles, Quartiles, and Stanines

Decile. A decile is any one of the nine points that divide a distribution into ten parts, each containing one-tenth of all the scores. The first decile is the tenth percentile, the eighth decile, the eightieth percentile, etc. (Every tenth percentile along a normal curve.)

Quartile. A quartile is any one of three points that divide the subjects into four equal parts. The middle quartile is the same as the 50th percentile (or median). The third quartile sets off the top fourth, or 75th percentile. The first 25th percentile defines the lowest one-fourth of the subjects.

Stanine. The word stanine was derived from two words, *standard nine*. Therefore, it is defined as any one of the steps in a nine-point scale of standard scores. The stanine has values from one to nine, with a mean of five and a standard deviation of two. Each stanine (except one and nine) is one-half standard deviation in width. The middle stanine (five), extends from one-fourth standard deviation below the mean to one-fourth standard deviation above the mean.

Statistical Significance

Significance levels refer to the risk of error we are willing to take in drawing conclusions from data.

In psychological research, it is often necessary to generalize from a particular sample to a larger population. There are statistical procedures for estimating probable fluctuation to expect from sample to sample in the size of correlations, means, standard deviations and other group measures.

In correlations the question often asked is if the correlation is significantly greater than zero. When we say that a correlation is "significant at the one percent (.01) level" it means the chances are no greater than one out of 100 that the population correlation is zero. The variables are related.

Minimum correlations significant at the .01 and .05 levels for groups of different sizes can be found by consulting tables of the significance of correlations in statistics textbooks.

If two means are significant at the .01 level, this indicates that with one chance out of 100 of being wrong, that a difference in the obtained direction would be found if we tested the whole population from which the samples are drawn.

Grade Equivalent

Grade equivalent (GE) expresses a score using the grade levels, 1-12 (as in the school systems), as units of measurement. This simple term is useful but it is often over-used and misinterpreted. The school year is divided into tenths and GE's may be interpreted thereby; 4.5 — work equivalent of a normal youngster half way through the fourth grade; 6.2 — equal to work expected of a sixth grade child after two-tenths or one-fifth of the sixth grade has been completed.

There are some weaknesses in the utilization of GE's. For example, a child who scores 4.5 in reading on an achievement test may have specific reading deficiencies which the teacher needs to know about. The 4.5 does not tell us whether the child is stronger in silent or oral reading and says nothing about work attack skills, auditory versus visual skills, etc.

Standard Error of Measurement

The standard error of measurement is a statistical procedure for quantifying reliability when reliability data have been gathered. It examines the variability found with repeated measures. Examiners can compute standard deviations to describe variability, if the measurement is repeated a number of times with a single subject and the distribution of the repeated measurements are examined.

Synonymous terms are "standard error," "test error" and "error of measurement." The standard error of measurement of a test indicates the extent that chance errors cause variations in the scores obtained by an individual if the same test were administered an infinite number of times. Tests with a relatively small standard error are much more desirable than tests with a relatively large standard error.

Correlation

Correlation refers to how two or more characteristics are associated or related and what they have in common. These characteristics are called variables, and can be changed, manipulated, controlled, and/or observed by the person conducting the experiment.

When addressing the term correlation, the terms positive correlation and negative correlation are often referred to. Positive correlation is obtained when a large amount of one variable is associated with a large amount of another variable. Or it may be positively correlated when a small amount of one variable is associated with a small amount of another variable.

> *Example*: Teachers observe that students who have high intelligence quotients tend to receive high scores in mathematics tests; whereas those with low IQ's tend to score low.

Negative correlations are obtained when a large amount of one variable is associated with a small amount of the other. As one increases, the other will decrease.

> *Example*: As a student's anxiety level concerning taking tests increases, the scores he obtains on tests may

tend to decrease.

Actually, the word *correlation* describes a relationship which exists between two variables. The *coefficient of correlation* describes the degree of relationship that exists between characteristics and scores and sets of scores. You may obtain a perfect positive relationship (+ 1.0) or a perfect negative relationship (− 1.0). Ordinarily, a correlation of + .75 or above, or − .75 or below is considered a very high correlation.

Reliability

Reliability can be defined as the degree of consistency between two measures of the same thing. Any measurement device only provides a very limited amount of data. What we would hope is that a person's score would be similar under slightly different conditions. For example, if we measure a person's weight, we would hope that we would have gotten almost the same measure had we used a different scale or weighed him one day later. If we were going to measure a person's level of achievement, we would hope that his score would be similar under different administrators, using different scorers, with similar but not identical items, or during a different time of day.

Reliability involves the stability or consistency of test scores obtained by an individual when successive measures are taken with the same instrument or equivalent test forms.

Validity

The validity of a test refers to the extent to which a test measures what it is supposed to measure. The test must be valid for the particular purposes for which it is being used or the results cannot be used with any degree of confidence. There are four types of validity: content validity, criterion-related validity, concurrent validity and predictive validity.

Content validity involves the careful evaluation of the content of the test in order to determine if the items are representative of that which they purport to measure. Content validity can be built into a test by selecting only those items that measure a trait or behavior or interest. Naturally, it is one of the most important points in the development of any educational or psychological test.

Criterion validity refers to the relationship between test scores and some type of outcome. The criterion should be readily measurable, free from bias, and relevant to the purposes of the test.

Concurrent validity refers to whether the test scores are related to some currently available criterion measure. Concurrent validity should be used with tests to measure existing status but not for predicting future outcomes.

Predictive validity refers to the correlation between test scores and performance on a relevant criterion where there is a time lapse between test administration and performance on the criterion. In other words, predictive validity involves testing the effectiveness of a test against future performance in an area or areas purportedly measured by the test.

Population, Sampling, Parameters

We use the term population to refer to an entire group or the total number from which samples are taken for a particular purpose.

Most methods of sampling are designed to obtain a small sample which represents a much larger population. The population may be tested, observed, surveyed, or whatever is appropriate for that situation.

When we test an entire population and then characterize or describe the population in terms of particular properties, these properties would be called *parameters*.

Item Analysis

When one analyzes individual items on a test it is called *item analysis*. There are several different ways to analyze individual items and there are several different purposes for analyzing items. The objective generally is to learn of the difficulty of the item. Many times though, the items will be analyzed to determine how well they discriminate between such factors as knowledge, ability, those who are likely to succeed and those who will not. Some item analyses involve a very complex statistical analysis while other procedures are not so strict.

Glossary of Measurement Terms

Adaptive behavior. The ability to cope with the demands of the environment; includes self-help, communication, and social skills.

Age equivalent. The age for which a given test score is the real or estimated average; reported in years and months.

Age norms. Values representing typical or average performance for persons of various age groups.

Alternate-form reliability. The closeness of correspondence, or correlation, between results on alternate forms of a test; thus a measure of the extent to which the two forms are consistent in measuring whatever they do measure.

Arithmetic mean. The sum of a set of scores divided by the number of scores.

Assessment. The process of gathering information for the purpose of making educational decisions.

Basal. In test administration, the point at which it can be assumed that the student would receive credit for all easier test items.

Ceiling. In test administration, the point at which it can be assumed that the student would not get credit for all the more difficult test items.

Checklists. An informal assessment device that allows an informant to quickly scan lists of descriptions and to check those which apply to the student in question.

Chronological Age (CA). The number of years and months since birth.

Comprehension skills. In reading, the ability to understand what is read; may be assessed via silent or oral reading.

Computation skills. In math, verbal and written addition, multiplication, subtraction, and division of whole numbers, fractions, and decimals.

Correlation coefficient. A statistic that indicates the degree of relationship between two sets of scores.

Criterion-referenced tests. An informal assessment device that compares the student's performance on the curriculum rather than to the performance of other children.

Diagnostic test. A test used to locate specific areas of weakness or strength, and to determine the nature of weaknesses or deficiencies; most commonly prepared for the skill subjects—reading, writing, and math.

Distribution. A tabulation of scores from high to low, or low to high, showing the number of individuals that obtained each score or fall into each score interval.

Due process. Procedural safeguards established to insure that the rights of exceptional students and their parents are not violated.

Error analysis. A type of work sample analysis that describes and categorizes the incorrect responses of the student.

Formal assessment. Assessment procedures that contain specific rules for administration, scoring, and interpretation; these tests are generally norm referenced and/or standardized.

Grade equivalent. The grade level for which a given score is the real or estimated average; expressed in grades and tenths of grades (eg. 4.5 = fourth grade, fifth month).

Group test. A test which is administered to more than one student at a time.

Individual test. A test which can be administered to only one person at a time.

Individualized Educational Program (IEP). A written education plan developed for each student eligible for special education. Contains long-range goals and short term objectives specifically designed for the student.

Informal assessment. Assessment procedures without rigid administration, scoring, and interpretation rules; includes criterion-referenced tests, task analysis, inventories, etc.

Intelligence. The ability of an individual to understand and cope with the environment; generally measured by intelligence or IQ tests which predict academic aptitude.

Intelligence quotient. Originally, the ratio of a person's mental age (MA) to his chronological age (CA).

$$IQ = \frac{\text{Mental Age}}{\text{Chronological Age}} \times 100$$

Least restrictive environment. According to PL 94-142, the educational placement for handicapped students that is as close to the regular class setting as possible.

Mean. See*Arithmetic mean.*

Median. The middle score in a distribution; the 50th percentile; the point that divides the group into two equal parts. Half of the group fall below the median and half above it.

Mental Age (MA). The age for which a given score on an intelligence test is average.

Mode. The score which occurs most often in a distribution of scores; a measure of central tendency. In a normal curve the Mean, Median, and Mode are equal.

N. The symbol commonly used to represent the number of cases or scores in a distribution, study, etc.

Norm-referenced standardized test. A test that compares a student's performance to that of the students in the norm group.

Norms. Statistics that describe the test performance of specified groups, such as pupils of various ages or grades in the standardization group for a test. Norms are often assumed to be representative of some larger population.

Normal distribution. A distribution of scores or measures that in graphic form has a distinctive bell-shaped appearance. In a normal distribution, scores are distributed symmetrically about the mean, with as many cases at various distances above the mean as at equal distances below it, and with cases concentrated near the average.

Objective test. A test in the scoring of which there is no possibility of a difference of opinion among scorers as to whether responses are to be scored right or wrong.

Percentile. A point (score) in a distribution below which falls the percent of cases indicated by the given percentile. Thus the forty-fifth percentile denotes the score or point below which forty-five per cent of the scores fall. Percentile has nothing to do with the percent of correct answers an examinee has on a test.

Percentile rank score. A score that translates a student's test performance into the percentage of norm group students that performed as well as, or poorer than, that student on the same test.

Practice effect. The influence of previous experience with a test on later administration of the same test or a similar test.

Projective technique. A method of personality study in which the subject responds as he chooses to a series of stimuli such as pictures, ink-blots, unfinished sentences, etc.

Rating scale. An informal assessment device in which the informant judges or rates the performance of the student.

Random sample. A sample of the members of the population drawn in such a way that every member of the population has an equal chance of being included — that is, drawn in such a way as to prevent bias. Very difficult to design a true random sample.

Range. The difference between the lowest and highest scores obtained on a test by some group.

Raw score. The first score calculated, usually indicates the number of correct responses on a test or subtest.

Reliability. The extent to which a test is *consistent* in measuring whatever it does measure; *dependability*, *stability*, relative errors of measurement.

Standardized test. A systematic sample of performance obtained under prescribed conditions, scored according to definite rules, and capable of evaluation by reference to normative information.

Task analysis. An informal assessment technique in which a task is broken into a list of subtasks and its essential components.

Validity. The extent to which a test does the job for which it is used.

CHAPTER 4

TESTING INSTRUMENTS AND DEVICES
IN THE PROCESS OF ASSESSMENT

A LARGE number of measurement tools have been used widely in the evaluation of children. The tests selected for review here are of value to evaluate a large proportion of the population.

The Stanford-Binet and the Wechsler tests are discussed first because they are the most often used in terms of individual mental measurement. Many of the tests are accompanied by reproductions of test face sheets which the author hopes will help the reader visualize the test content and structure.

Wechsler Intelligence Scale for Children Revised (WISC-R)

The WISC-R is designed to measure several aspects of general intelligence. The WISC-R includes twelve subtests that emphasize various types of ability. These subtests contribute to the composite of intellectual functioning.

The WISC-R is divided into two major categories: Verbal and Performance. Intelligence quotients are calculated on five verbal and five performance subtests. Each of these scales has five subtests and one supplementary or alternate subtest. The five subtests are mandatory, but the alternates are to be given when time allows or if

A small portion of this chapter is adapted from the following work: Love, Harold D., *Teaching Mildly Handicapped Children — Methods and Materials*, Charles C Thomas, Publisher, 1984.

a regularly administered test is invalidated or cannot be properly administered. The use of the subtests can add useful qualitative and diagnostic information. The following order is recommended; however, the examiner is free to change it to meet the needs of the testing situation:

Verbal Scale	Performance Scale
1. Information	2. Picture Completion
3. Similarities	4. Picture Arrangement
5. Arithmetic	6. Block Design
7. Vocabulary	8. Object Assembly
9. Comprehension	10. Coding (or Mazes)
11. Digit Span	12. Mazes (Supplement
(Supplement or alternate)	or alternate)

The WISC-R is appropriate for children six through seventeen years of age. Because of the age discrepancy in subjects, different starting points have been specified for each subtest depending on the subject's age and estimated ability. The directions for starting and stopping are indicated in the manual and on the record form. Basal levels must be established in order to assume credit for easier items not given. Rules in the manual give guidelines for basal levels for each subtest.

Test materials for the WISC-R are contained in a briefcase kit. It includes a manual, individual record forms, cards, blocks, puzzles and booklets for the various subtests. The examiner provides a stopwatch for timing.

Each subtest is arranged in order of increasing difficulty. In scoring the WISC-R, raw scores are transformed into scaled scores for the subject's age group. Tables of scores are provided for four month intervals between six years and sixteen years and eleven months. The scaled subtests have a distribution with a mean of ten and standard deviation of three. So a score of ten on a subtest is average. A score of seven is one standard deviation below the mean for a given age. After the subtests are scaled they are combined to form an overall verbal I.Q. score, and overall performance I.Q. score and these are combined to form the full scale I.Q. score.

WISC-R RECORD FORM

Wechsler Intelligence Scale for Children—Revised

NAME Wm. Carter AGE 9 SEX M

ADDRESS Acorn, AR

PARENT'S NAME Jack + Florine

SCHOOL Jake Elem. GRADE 4th

PLACE OF TESTING Office TESTED BY Flea

REFERRED BY Miss Simms

WISC-R PROFILE

Clinicians who wish to draw a profile should first transfer the child's scaled scores to the row of boxes below. Then mark an X on the dot corresponding to the scaled score for each test, and draw a line connecting the X's.*

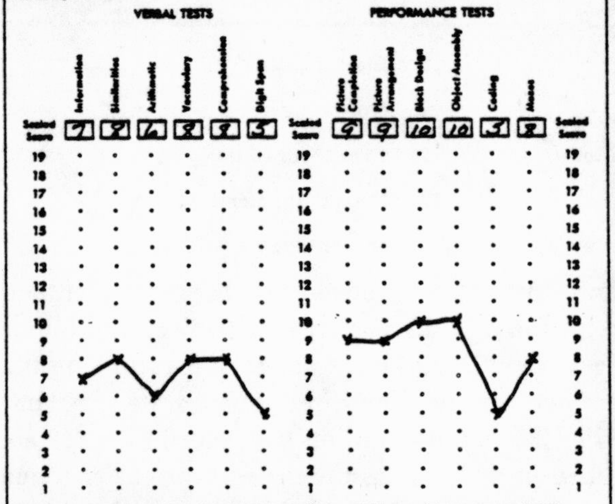

*See Chapter 4 in the manual for a discussion of the significance of differences between scores on the tests.

	Year	Month	Day
Date Tested	83	2	9
Date of Birth	74	2	8
Age	9	o	1

	Raw Score	Scaled Score
VERBAL TESTS		
Information	10	7
Similarities	9	8
Arithmetic	8	6
Vocabulary	22	8
Comprehension	11	8
(Digit Span)	(6)	(5)
Verbal Score		37
PERFORMANCE TESTS		
Picture Completion	17	10
Picture Arrangement	19	9
Block Design	22	10
Object Assembly	20	10
Coding	22	5
(Mazes)	(16)	(8)
Performance Score		44

	Scaled Score	IQ
Verbal Score	37	84
Performance Score	44	91
Full Scale Score	81	86

*Prorated from 4 tests, if necessary.

NOTES

left handed
hyper
bites nails
hates School
attention getter
poor memory
has trouble expressing himself.

Short Attention Span

WRAT
Spelling 1.6
Word Attack 1.1
Arith. 2.6
Woodcock
Total Reading 1.3

Figure 4.1.

The following is a list of skills measured by the WISC-R:

Verbal Tests

INFORMATION
Common everyday experiences and things learned at school.

SIMILARITIES
Ability to discriminate likenesses and verbalize appropriate relationships between two ostensibly dissimilar objects or concepts.

ARITHMETIC
Manipulate number concepts. Ability to reason using simple numerical operations.

VOCABULARY
General intelligence. Abstract thinking. Manipulation of verbal signs and symbols.

COMPREHENSION
Child's comprehension of social and/or moral behavioral development.

(DIGIT SPAN)
Rote memory. Auditory sequencing.

Performance Tests

PICTURE COMPLETION
Visual attention and visual concentration.

PICTURE ARRANGEMENT
Perception, visual comprehension and sequential planning are necessary skills.

BLOCK DESIGN
Ability to perceive, analyze, synthesize and reproduce abstract designs.

OBJECT ASSEMBLY
Synthesis of parts into an organized integrated whole.

CODING
Visual-motor dexterity. Pencil manipulation. Speed and accuracy in making association.

(MAZES)
Ability to plan ahead, organization, motor and visual integration.

Wechsler Preschool and Primary Scale of Intelligence (WPPSI)

The WPPSI is used with children between four and six and a half years of age. Four different Wechsler Intelligence Scales are widely used in the public schools by certified psychologists. The main difference between the scales is the age group for which it is intended. The Wechsler Intelligence Scale for Children used to be the most widely used individual intelligence test for children five to fifteen years of age. It has primarily been replaced by the WPPSI and WISC-R. The Wechsler Adult Intelligence Scale — Revised is used to test the general intelligence of persons between the ages of sixteen and seventy-four.

The Coding subtest on the WISC-R is called Digit Symbol on the WAIS-R and Animal House on the WPPSI. There are two subtests which appear on the WPPSI and not on the others. They are:

SENTENCES

It assesses the ability to repeat sentences verbatim.

GEOMETRIC DESIGN

This subtest assesses the ability to copy geometric designs.

Stanford-Binet Intelligence Scale

The Stanford-Binet Intelligence Scale 1960 revision is recommended with subjects from two years of age through adulthood. The test is seldom used in school systems for children older than ten or twelve because of the time involved in administering it. In cases of children over ten or twelve, the WISC-R or WAIS-R is normally used. The Stanford-Binet contains a series of items, increasing in difficulty, grouped by age level beginning at age two and progressing to adulthood. There are six test items and an alternate item for each age level, with the exception of the average adult level, which has eight items and an alternate item. Test items appearing at each age level are shown in Table 4.1 and the table suggests the number of months given toward the subject's mental age (MA). The MA is determined by adding to the basal age the month of credit earned above the basal age. Deviation I.Q.'s are computed from standard scores on an assumed mean of 100 and a standard deviation of sixteen.

WPPSI **RECORD FORM**

Wechsler Preschool and Primary Scale of Intelligence

NAME Anita AGE 5 SEX F

ADDRESS

PARENT'S NAME

SCHOOL Fair Park GRADE K

PLACE OF TESTING Spec. Serv. Ofc. TESTED BY H. Jones

REFERRED BY Jane Meadows (Teacher)

NOTES

Right handed
Talkative (very)
Father - farmer
Mother - factory worker
Middle Child.

hyperactive
good rapport established

	Year	Month	Day
Date Tested	83	10	6
Date of Birth	78	6	7
Age	5	3	23

	Raw Score	Scaled Score
VERBAL TESTS		
Information	14	11
Vocabulary	15	9
Arithmetic	12	12
Similarities	17	16
Comprehension	16	11
(Sentences)	-	-
Verbal Score		59
PERFORMANCE TESTS		
Animal House	40	10
Picture Completion	10	9
Mazes	9	9
Geometric Design	12	13
Block Design	4	7
(Animal House Retest)	-	-
Performance Score		48

	Scaled Score	IQ
Verbal Score	59	111
Performance Score	48	97
Full Scale Score	107	105

*Prorated if necessary

Printed in U.S.A. 77-153AS

Figure 4.2.

TABLE 4.1

Age Levels for Stanford-Binet test items

Age level		Number of items plus alternate (A)	Months added to MA for each item passed
Years	Months		
2	0	6 plus A	Subject must pass all items for the test to be valid
2	6	6 plus A	1 month
3	0	6 plus A	1 month
3	6	6 plus A	1 month
4	0	6 plus A	1 month
4	6	6 plus A	1 month
5		6 plus A	2 months
6		6 plus A	2 months
7		6 plus A	2 months
8		6 plus A	2 months
9		6 plus A	2 months
10		6 plus A	2 months
11		6 plus A	2 months
12		6 plus A	2 months
13		6 plus A	2 months
14		6 plus A	2 months
Average Adult		8 plus A	2 months
Superior Adult I		6 plus A	4 months
Superior Adult II		6 plus A	5 months
Superior Adult III		6 plus A	6 months

Kaufman Assessment Battery for Children (K-ABC)

The authors conclude that five years of intensive research reached culmination in the official publication of the K-ABC on April 4, 1983. The K-ABC is a clinical instrument for the evaluation of pre-school and elementary school children. Developed from recent research and theory in neuropsychology and cognitive psychology, the K-ABC assesses the ability to solve problems using simultaneous and sequential mental processes. In addition the K-ABC has a separate Achievement Scale which measures a child's acquired knowledge, including skills in reading and math. The authors claim that the Achievement Scale provides a frame of reference for evaluating the extent to which children have been able to apply their mental processing skills to a variety of learning situations.

The K-ABC is an individually administered measure of intelligence and achievement for children ages two and a half through twelve and a half years. This instrument is a multisubtest battery yielding scores in four global areas of functioning: Sequential Processing, Mental Processing, Simultaneous Processing, Mental Processing Composite (Sequential plus Simultaneous), and Achievement. There are sixteen subtests although a maximum of thirteen are administered to any particular child.

American Guidance Service says that the K-ABC is the only major intelligence test to use a norm group stratified using 1980 census data. The norming sample included representative proportions of Whites, Blacks, Hispanics, Asians and Native Americans. The publisher also tells us that exceptional children were systematically included in the K-ABC standardization sample in representative proportions.

The authors also conclude that factor analytic investigations demonstrate strong evidence of content validity. About forty validity studies have been conducted to data testing a wide variety of normal and exceptional populations and show evidence of construct, concurrent, and predictive validity.

Reliability coefficients, using the split-half methods, for the global scales are reported by the authors to be:

Pre-school ages   .86-.93
Elementary ages   .89-.97

Slosson Intelligence Test

The Slosson Intelligence Test (SIT) is a relatively short screening test which was designed to evaluate mental ability. The test includes many items that appear in the Stanford-Binet Intelligence Scale. The test is designed to be administered by teachers, counselors, principals, psychologists, school nurses and other people who in their professional work need to evaluate an individual's mental ability. Items on this test range from the .5 month level to the twenty-seven year level; however, the author does not report an age range for individuals who may be evaluated with this test. There are directions in the manual about testing infants, those who have reading handicaps or language handicaps, the blind, hard of hearing, those with organic brain damage, the emotionally disturbed and the deprived.

The raw score on the SIT is an age score. An individual earns a specific number of months credit for each item answered correctly. Those items between the basal and the ceiling are the only ones administered. The age score is then transformed into a ratio I.Q.

Nebraska Test of Learning Aptitude

The Nebraska Test of Learning Aptitude (NTLA) by Hiskey (1966) is an individually administered test designed to assess the learning aptitude of deaf and hearing individuals between three and sixteen years of age. This test has twelve subtests with instructions for pantomime administration of the test for deaf children and verbal instructions for use with children who can hear. Because of that, if pantomime directions are used, the scoring must be based on the norms for deaf children. Also, if verbal directions are used the scoring must be based on the norms for hearing children.

Each subtest is a power test beginning with very simple items which are designed to give the child practice as he goes about the task. The response requirements are nonverbal and require the child to point in order to choose a correct item or a motor response such as stringing beads or drawing parts of pictures. Some subtests are administered to all ages, some are administered to children eleven years and older, and some are administered only to three to ten year olds.

The NTLA is a point scale; that is, a child earns points on each specific subtest that is presented to him. Different subtests employ different ceiling rules.

The kinds of scores obtained depend on how the test is administered. If the test is administered in pantomime the norms for deaf children are used to get a learning age (LA) and a learning quotient (LQ). If the test is administered verbally the norms for hearing children are used to get a mental age (MA) and an intelligence quotient (IQ). Hiskey warns that the LA and LQ for deaf children are not the same as the MA's and IQ's for hearing children.

McCarthy Scales of Children's Abilities

The McCarthy Scales of Children's Abilities was developed for children between the ages of two and a half and eight and a half years of age and has eighteen tests grouped into six overlapping scales. The scales include the verbal, percental-performance, quantitative, general cognitive, memory and motor. It appears that the general cognitive comes closest to the traditional global measure of intelligence. The behaviors sampled by the subtests include block building, puzzle solving, right-left orientation, leg coordination, arm coordination, imitative action, drawing a design, drawing a child, numerical memory, verbal fluency, counting and sorting, opposite analogies, and conceptual grouping.

Bayley Scales of Infant Development

The Bayley Scales of Infant Development is designed to yield a three part evaluation of a child's developmental status during the first two and a half years of life. Bayley states that: "The primary value of the development index is to provide that basis for establishing a child's current status, and thus the extent of any deviation from normal expectancy" (1969, p. 4).

The Mental Scale assesses sensory-perceptual acuities, discrimination, and the ability to respond to the early acquisition of "object permanency and memory, learning and problem solving ability, vocalization and early evidence of the ability to generalizations and classifications which are the basis of abstract thinking. Results are expressed as a standard score, the MDI, or Mental Development Index" (Bayley, 1969, p.3).

Woodcock-Johnson Psycho-Educational Battery

The Woodcock-Johnson Psycho-Educational Battery is a comprehensive set of twenty-seven subtests measuring cognitive abilities, scholastic aptitudes, achievement, and interests at preschool through adulthood. The tests are administered orally and to one person at a time.

The entire battery may be administered in one two-hour session. Raw scores are converted into meaningful information. The examiner may get grade scores, age scores, standard scores and percentile ranks. Salvia and Ysseldyke (1978) suggest that this test is extremely suitable for use with special education populations.

Cattell Infant Intelligence Scale

The Cattell Infant Intelligence Scale is a downward extension of the Stanford-Binet. The test has five test items at each month through twelve months, and at two month intervals to thirty months. At the low levels the tasks are such things as being attentive to voice, following a person with the eyes, following a dangling ring with the eyes, and head lifting. At an older level there is block building and manipulating spoons, cups, pegboards and formboards.

Leiter International Performance Scale

Leiter created his International Performance Test based on the premise that the ability to cope with a new situation is an indication of intelligence. (All information found in this part of the chapter, unless otherwise stated, is from Leiter's 1966 test manual.) The first test was created in 1927 and was only a fourteen notch frame. In 1928 and 1929 eleven tests were added. By 1930 a point system was devised for scoring and there were forty-four tests in all. The test was revised in 1936 to cover age five through sixteen. In 1938 another revision was made. This time the test ranged from three to twenty-two, twelve through twenty-two even years only. There were four subtests for each age.

These tests were developed during Dr. Leiter's work in Hawaii and standardized on Chinese and Japanese children there. The 1938 scale was tested by many others in the field. Anne Craig and H.S. Molino tested it using 286 Mexican children and H.E. Darby and L.J. Goulard tested the 1938 scale on Japanese American children born in California.

In 1940 the scale was revised again so it would be more useful in psychological clinics. The test now ranged from two through eighteen continuous, with four subtests at each age level. The last revision was in 1948. The main reason for the revision was to have the tests after ten at even years only. There were also a few changes at the lower end to make the test material the same as that used for the Arthur Adaptation.

Buros' Mental Measurement Yearbook No. 4 (1953) critiques Leiter's test. Several disadvantages were listed. First, the test requires a lot of expensive material. Second, the tests at level two and three years are too hard, the total scores of these levels average ten IQ points lower than other comparable scores. Third, validity for several subtests is questioned. The subtests in question are:

1. year V test 1 genus, subject may match for color
2. year V test 3 clothing, pictures out of style
3. 6 year tests seem to have sharp increase in difficulty level
4. year X test 1 footprints, not culturally appropriate
5. year XII test 2 similarities, the use of pictures, material, and real objects is confusing
6. year XII test 3 facial expression, other studies have indicated the unreliability of this type of test

Goodenough-Harris Draw-A-Man Test

The Goodenough-Harris Drawing Test is designed to test the intelligence of children between the ages of five through fifteen. It may be used for screening and is fast, nonthreatening, a means of gaining a good impression of a child's mental maturity. It is also a nonverbal test and can be used with bilingual and disadvantaged children. The child draws a picture of a man, a woman, and a "self" drawing. In the directions the child is asked to draw the very best picture he can of a man, a woman, and himself or herself. The test may be administered either as a group or individual test.

The scoring is not based on artistic skills, but on the presence of essential details and their relationship with each other. Credit is given for the inclusion of body parts, clothing details, proportion and perspective. Scoring items is done on the basis of age differentiation and relates to the total score on the test. There are seventy-three scorable items on the man scale and seventy-one items on the woman scale.

The author has used this test for many years and has found its best use is for screening young mentally retarded and gifted children.

Picture Vocabulary Tests

Peabody Picture Vocabulary Test — Revised

The Peabody Picture Vocabulary Test — Revised (PPVT-R) is an individually administered test designed to measure verbal intelligence through receptive vocabulary. This test, and all others like it, measure only one aspect of intelligence; receptive vocabulary. The PPVT-R is much better standardized than the old Peabody Picture Vocabulary Test and its technical characteristics far surpass those of other picture vocabulary tests. It is a very good screening device and inexperienced individuals may overgeneralize its utility.

Quick Test

The Quick Test is described by its authors as "the little brother of the Full Range Picture Vocabulary Test (FRPV), one of the most widely used brief tests of intelligence" (Ammons and Ammons, 1962, p. i). The Quick Test has three forms, each consisting of one plate of four drawings and words which the examiner reads. The authors state that each form of the test can be administered in two minutes or less.

Raw scores on the Quick Test consist of the number of correct responses between the basal and the ceiling. The raw scores may be transformed to MAs and ratio IQs.

The Full Range Picture Vocabulary Test

The Full Range Picture Vocabulary Test is designed to assess the intelligence of individuals from two years of age through adulthood. There are thirteen plates with four pictures on each plate, and a one page manual with norms printed on the back. This test has been around a long time and has been criticized because the norms were based only on 589 representative cases (Ammons & Ammons, 1948). The authors answer the criticism thusly:

> Critics of the FRPV not familiar with its widespread use and our extensive research program have implied or stated that the FRPV is "poorly standardized," etc. Actually, this is not the case. Rather, since shortly after the FRPV was made available for use, there has been so much research with it that we have not been able to keep up with the findings. One of the consequences of this widespread use has been that we have been unable to prepare a comprehensive manual, although many separate articles, reporting various aspects of work with the FRPV, have been published, we deliberately refrained from releasing the QT until this manual was ready, reporting all experience and known research to date. If our experience with the FRPV is any indication, we may never get caught up again (p. i.).

Visual-Motor Perceptual Tests

Bender Visual Motor Gestalt Test

The Bender Visual Motor Gestalt Test was developed by Lauretta Bender in 1938 as a means of investigating the applicability of the concepts of Gestalt psychology to the study of brain damage. The designs were among those used by Wertheimer (1923) in his studies of perception. Koppitz (1963) noted that most of the research

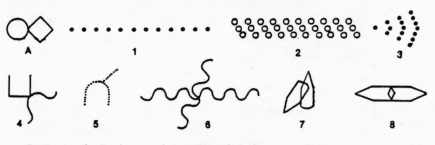

Designs on the Bender Visual Motor Gestalt Test.

Figure 4.3.

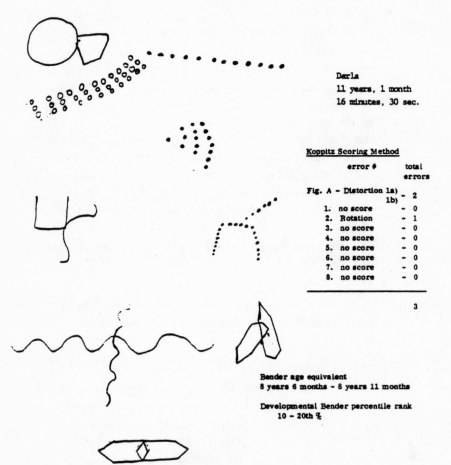

Darla
11 years, 1 month
16 minutes, 30 sec.

Koppitz Scoring Method

	error #	total errors
Fig. A – Distortion 1a) 1b)		– 2
1. no score		– 0
2. Rotation		– 1
3. no score		– 0
4. no score		– 0
5. no score		– 0
6. no score		– 0
7. no score		– 0
8. no score		– 0

3

Bender age equivalent
8 years 6 months – 8 years 11 months

Developmental Bender percentile rank
10 – 20th %

Figure 4.4

done on the Bender concerning children was published after 1955. Koppitz (1975) regarded the BVMGT a measure of visual-motor integration with a great deal of emphasis on integration.

The BVMGT is a visual motor test, consisting of nine figures, which are presented one at a time and which the subject is asked to copy on a blank piece of paper. Bender (1938) pointed out that the perception and reproduction of the Gestalt figures are determined by biological principles of sensory motor action and vary depending on (a) the growth pattern and maturation level of an individual, and (b) his pathological state either functionally or organically induced.

Bender's work was mainly devoted to adult patients suffering from organic brain disease, schizophrenia, depressive psychosis, psychoneurosis, and mental retardation, but Bender did not provide an objective scoring system for the test.

As the test was more widely used, the need for an objective scoring system became greater. Several were published, but the most widely accepted scoring system was that of Pascal and Suttell (1951). It was designed for adults fifteen to twenty years old. They caution using it with young children, and do not consider it reliable for children under nine years old.

Elizabeth M. Koppitz (1963) developed the scoring system for children ages five to ten years regardless of their intelligence, and up to sixteen years old for mentally retarded children whose mental age is ten years or less. The aim of the volume by Koppitz is to provide different ways of analyzing the Bender records of young children so that an examiner can evaluate their perceptual maturity, possible neurological impairment, and emotional adjustment from a single Bender Test protocol.

It seems clear that the Bender Test is related to intelligence in children, but once visual motor perception has fully matured — at age nine most children can execute the test without serious error — it can no longer serve as a measure of intellectual ability. Therefore, the Bender Test can help predict school achievement. Also, several deviations on the test are diagnostically significant for brain injury. The Bender Test is an important aid in the study of mental retardation, with its greatest value being its use as a test of mental maturity and as an indicator of academic achievement level of retarded children. The Bender Test is also used with children with emotional disturbances.

Administration of the test consists of seating the child comfortably at an uncluttered table, on which two sheets of paper and a pencil with eraser have been placed. Be sure that the child is well rested. After rapport has been established, show the child the stack of Bender cards and say, "I have nine cards here with designs on them for you to copy. Here is the first one. Now go ahead and make one just like it." When the child has finished drawing the figure the card is removed and the next one is placed in front of him until all nine cards are presented in this fashion and orderly sequence. If the child asks questions, give him a noncommittal answer such as, "Make it look as much like the picture on the card as you can." Do not discourage erasures or several attempts at drawing a design. You may, however, discourage counting dots by telling the child that it is not necessary. If he needs more paper, give it to him. There is no time limit, although a record should be kept of the time required.

Frostig Developmental Test of Visual Perception

The Frostig Developmental Test of Visual Perception (DTVP) was developed in 1963 by Marianne Frostig as an aid in differentiating the visual perceptual disabilities. The test seeks to measure five operationally defined perceptual skills: Subtest 1, Eye-Motor Coordination (16 items); Subtest 2, Figure-Ground (8 items); Subtest 3, Constancy of Shape (17 items); Subtest 4, Position in Space (8 items); Subtest 5, Spatial Relations (8 items)l

The test was designed for use with children three to eight years of age, although there are special scoring instructions for children over eight. The DTVP has an advantage over many other perceptual tests in that it may be administered either individually or in groups up to thirty.

Administration of the test requires that the examiner be thoroughly familiar with the manual and the testing procedures in order to insure test validity. Frostig recommends that handicapped or severely emotionally disturbed children should be given the test individually and only by an experienced psychologist since testing rapport is an important variable that could affect performance. The test requires minimum use of language, and a special adaptation of the administration manual is available from the publisher for use with deaf, hard-of-hearing, and non-English speaking children. Time required for administration is about thirty to forty-five minutes for individual administration and forty to sixty minutes with group administrations.

Test materials include a thirty-five page test booklet, the back cover of which is designed to serve as a score sheet and as a record of personal information; a revised administration and scoring manual (1966, 38 pages), eleven demonstration cards, three scoring keys, and a monograph on the 1963 standardization procedure (1964, 37 pages). In addition, depending upon the age level of the child or group, the examiner must provide colored pencils or crayons in contrasting colors (red, blue, brown, and green are recommended) or No. 2 pencils without erasers and a blackboard or portable slate for demonstration purposes.

Examiners are cautioned to make sure that each child's work surface is smooth as any cracks or ridges can interfere with performance and scoring. In addition, each child's work area should be free of all other material except the test materials, pencils must be well-sharpened, and frequent rest breaks allowed for those children who appear to be hyperactive. All work is done from left to right regardless of the child's handedness.

Detailed directions for the administration of each subtest are given in the manual. The examiner instructs the child or children to draw or outline with a crayon, colored pencil or No. 2 pencil stimulus items in the test booklet. Use of crayons, colored pencils or No. 2 pencils depends upon the age level of the child or group and the subtest. Crayons are used for nursery school children while the colored or No. 2 pencils are used with children in kindergarten and above.

Detailed directions for scoring each subtest along with illustrated examples are also included in the manual. Three types of scores are provided and must be considered in conjunction with one another, rather than separately. Tables are provided in the manual for the conversion of raw data to these scores. Frostig (1966) describes these scores in the test manual in the following terms:

Perceptual Age. Perceptual age level is defined in terms of the performance of the average child in the corresponding age group for each subtest.

Scale Scores. Scale Scores are Perceptual Ages divided by Chronological Ages and multiplied by 10, adjusted to the nearest whole number:

$$\frac{PA}{CA} \times 10 = \text{Scale Score}$$

Perceptual Quotient. The Perceptual Quotient is a deviation score obtained from the sum of the subtest scale scores after correction for age variation. Unlike Scale Scores, however, it is not a ratio; it has been defined in terms of constant percentiles for each age group, with a median of 100, upper and lower quartiles of 110 and 90, respectively, and other percentile ranks consistent with I.Q. values of the Wechsler Intelligence Scale for Children (WISC).

The five perceptual age levels and the five scaled scores (one for each subtest) indicate the child's development in each visual perceptual ability. A scaled score of eight or below indicates that the child has below average ability in that area. Regarding the Perceptual Quotient, Frostig (1966) comments that research has indicated that children who fall in the lowest quartile at the age they begin school are likely to experience difficulty adjusting to school, and consequently, should have a well designed program of perceptual training.

Pupil Behavior Rating Scales

The American Association of Mental Deficiency (AAMD) Adaptive Behavior Scale

The AAMD is composed of 111 items covering twenty-four areas of social and personal behavior for use in evaluating effectiveness in coping with environmental demands. This scale aids in classifying mentally retarded individuals based on the way they maintain personal independence and meet social expectations. The scale is divided into two parts — one for children aged three to twelve and the other for children thirteen and older.

Burk's Behavior Rating Scales

The Burks' Behavior Rating Scales (BBRS) are specifically designed to identify patterns of pathological behavior shown in children who have been referred to school or community counseling agencies because of behavior problems in the school or home. The scales have 110 items which are used to gauge the severity of negative symptoms as seen by outside persons — usually teachers or parents.

The rater performs a quantitative judgment by determining the degree to which the following behaviors have been observed:

1. Excessive Self-Blame	11. Poor Impulse Control
2. Excessive Anxiety	12. Poor Reality Contact
3. Excessive Withdrawal	13. Poor Sense of Identity
4. Excessive Dependency	14. Excessive Suffering
5. Poor Ego Strength	15. Poor Anger Control
6. Poor Physical Strength	16. Excessive Sense of Persecution
7. Poor Coordination	17. Excessive Aggressiveness
8. Poor Intellectuality	18. Excessive Resistance
9. Poor Academics	19. Poor Social Conformity
10. Poor Attention	

Adaptive Behavior Inventory for Children (ABIC)

The ABIC is an adaptive behavior scale that measures six areas of adaptive behavior: Family, Peers, Community, School, Earner/Consumer, and Self-maintenance. Mercer and Lewis (1978) tell us that ABIC deals with the child's family life, peer relations in school, ability to function in a variety of settings and roles, types of activities engaged in during leisure time, and extent to which the child performs routine household chores.

Pupil Rating Scale

The Pupil Rating Scale was developed by Helmer R. Myklebust

and designed for use by regular classroom teachers for referring children suspected of being learning disabled. Five areas of behavior are observed: Auditory Comprehension, Spoken Language, Orientation, Motor Coordination, and Personal-Social Behavior. Precise statements of observable behavior are listed to which the teacher assigns a rating of 1, 2, 3, 4, or 5 (1 is the lowest, 5 the highest, and 3 is average). Low scores in a particular area or on the entire scale indicate a need for further diagnosis. The PRS can be used for screening children through the fourth grade and the screening device usually requires between fifteen to thirty minutes to administer.

Motor Proficiency Scales

Oseretsky Tests of Motor Proficiency

The Oseretsky Tests of Motor Proficiency originally were developed in Russia. Edgar A. Doll sponsored and edited an English translation from Portuguese. The OTMP can be administered individually or in groups. This device has six groups of tests for each age level tested. The tests include: General Static Coordination, Coordination of Hands, General Coordination, Motor Speed, Simultaneous Voluntary Movements, and Ability to Perform without Superfluous Movements. The OTMP may be used with children four through sixteen years of age.

Motor-Problems Inventory

The Motor-Problems Inventory by Glyndon D. Riley consists of fifteen motor tasks. These tasks fall under four descriptive categories: Gross Motor Coordination, Laterality, Small Motor Coordination, and General Observations. Scoring is done by circling appropriate numbers (0 indicates no problem, 2 indicates many problems) and adding these to derive a total score. Naturally, the total score indicates the degree of severity of the motor problem. The MPI may be administered to children ranging from pre-school to fifth grade and requires five to ten minutes to administer.

Achievement Tests

In all states an achievement test score is required before placement of the child in special services and periodic tests are administered during the placement period. Achievement tests are devices which directly assess a student's skill in academic content areas. These tests sample the products of past formal and informal educational experiences. They measure the extent to which a student has profited from schooling and life experiences compared to other children the same age.

There are so many achievement tests on the market which assess skills in reading, math and language that the author has chosen only one on which to elaborate.

California Achievement Test

The California Achievement Test (CAT) is a group administered, norm-referenced, multiple-skill assessment battery measuring skill development in many areas from grades 1.5 to 12. There are two forms of the test at each of five educational levels.

The CAT assesses skill development in three academic content areas: language, math and reading. Salvia and Ysseldyke (1978) state that the specific subtests sample the following behaviors:

Vocabulary. The student is required to select from four alternative response words the word with the same meaning as a stimulus word used in context. In addition, some items at levels 1 and 2 assess word skills such as sentence-picture association, beginning sounds, ending sounds, and word recognition.

Comprehension. The student must read sentences or passages and indicate comprehension of the material by answering multiple-choice questions.

Mathematics Computation. The student must solve computational problems of increasing difficulty.

Mathematics Concepts. The student must demonstrate knowledge and use of such concepts as forms of measurement, sequences, money, time, geometry, and place values.

Mathematics Problems. The student must comprehend and answer correctly a variety of work problems ranging from those involving basic one-step operations to those requiring two-step and three-step operations.

Language Mechanics. The student must capitalize and punctuate sentences and paragraphs.

Language Usage and Structure. The student must select which of four response possibilities best fits a blank in a sentence, thereby demonstrating knowledge of grammatical usage and structure.

Language Spelling. The student must select which of four response possibilities best fits a blank in a sentence, thereby demonstrating spelling knowledge.

Auditory Discrimination Tests

Wepman's Auditory Discrimination Tests

This test measures children's ability to hear accurately phonemes. The test consists of forty word-pairs matched for familiarity, length, and phonetic category. Ten of the word-pairs do not differ, while thirty word-pairs differ in a single phoneme (initial consonants, final consonants, or medial vowels). The examiner reads each pair, and the child must indicate whether the words are different or the same. The test comes in two forms and administration time is about five minutes.

The score is determined by the total number of correctly identified unidentical pairs. A five point scale is used to classify the scores.

Lindamood Auditory Conceptualization Test

The Lindamood Auditory Conceptualization Test (LACT) is an individually administered test designed to evaluate the child's ability to discriminate speech sounds and to perceive the number and order of sounds within a spoken pattern. The test is designed for use with kindergarten through twelfth grade children in the identification of auditory perceptual deficiencies. Two alternate forms of the test are available.

Goldman-Fristoe-Woodcock Test of Auditory Discrimination

The Goldman-Fristoe-Woodcock Test of Auditory Discrimination provides standardized measures of speech-sound discrimination ability for children and adults. Sattler (1982) states that the test has three parts:

1. **Training procedure.** During the training procedure the examinee is familiarized with the pictures and names that are used on the two subtests.
2. **Quiet Subtest.** Individual words are presented in the absence of any noise. This subtest provides a measure of auditory discrimination under ideal conditions.
3. **Noise Subtest.** The words are presented in the presence of a distracting "cafeteria" background noise on the tape. This subtest provides a measure of auditory discrimination under conditions similar to those encountered in everyday life.

This auditory skills test battery consists of four tests which measure a wide range of auditory skills in subjects from age four and upward. The tests and subtests are listed below. Test materials are taped.

GFW Auditory Skills Test Battery

GFW Auditory Selective Attention Tests
    Quiet Subtest (11 items)
    Fanlike Noise Subtest (33 items)
    Cafeteria Noise Subtest (33 items)
    Voice Subtest (33 items)
GFW Auditory Discrimination Tests
    Part I (100 items)
    Part II (100 items)
    Part III (100 items)
GFW Auditory Memory Tests
    Test 1 Recognition Memory (110 items)
    Test 2 Memory for Content (16 items)
    Test 3 Memory for Sequence (14 items)
GFW Sound-Symbol Tests

Test 1 Sound Mimicry (55 items)
Test 2 Sound Recognition (30 items)
Test 3 Sound Analysis (28 items)
Test 4 Sound Blending (33 items)
Test 5 Sound-Symbol Association (55 items)
Test 6 Reading of Symbols (70 items)
Test 7 Spelling of Sounds (50 items)

BIBLIOGRAPHY

Ammons, R.B. and Ammons, H.S.: *The Full Range Picture Vocabulary Test*. New Orleans, R.B. Ammons, 1948.
Ammons, R.B. and Ammons, H.S.: The Quick Test (QT): Provisional Manual. *Psychological Reports, 11*:111-116, 1962.
Bayley, N.: *Bayley Scales of Infant Development: Birth to Two Years*. New York, Psychological Corporation, 1969.
Bender, A.L.: A visual motor gestalt test and its clinical use. N.W.: *American Orthopsychiatric Assoc. Research Monograph*, No. 3, 1938.
Buros, O.K.: *The Fourth Mental Measurement Yearbook*. Highland Park, N.J., Gryphon Press, 1953.
Frostig, Marianne.: *Administration and Scoring Manual: Developmental Test of Visual Perception*. Palo Alto, Consulting Psychologists Press, 1966.
Hiskey, Marshall S.: *Nebraska Test of Learning Aptitude*. Lincoln, Union College Press, 1966.
Koppitz, Ellizabeth M.: *The Bender Gestalt Test for Young Children*. New York, Grune and Stratton, 1963.
Koppitz, Elizabeth M.: *The Bender Gestalt Test for Young Children (VII)*. New York, Grune and Stratton, 1975.
Leiter, Russell G.: *Evidences of the Reliability and Validity of the Leiter Tests*. Chicago, C.H. Stoeling Co., 1966.
Leiter, Russell G.: *General Instructions for the Leiter International Performance Scale*. Chicago, C.H. Stoeling Co., 1966.
Mercer, J.R. and Lewis, J.F.: *System of Multicultural Pluralistic Assessment*. New York, Psychological Corporation, 1978.
Pascal, G. and Suttell B.: *The Bender Gestalt Test*. New York, Grune and Stratton, 1951.
Salvia, John and Ysseldyke, James E.: *Assessment in Special and Remedial Education*. Boston, Houghton Mifflin Co., 1978.
Sattler, Jerome M.: *Assessment of Children's Intelligence and Special Abilities*, 2nd ed., Boston, Allyn & Bacon, 1982.

Wertheimer, M.: Studies in the theory of Gestalt psychology. *Psychology Forsch,* 4:300, 1923.

CHAPTER 5

OTHER TESTS AND ASSESSMENT TOOLS

IN Chapter Four the author provided a review of approximately thirty tests, devices, and educational techniques in educational assessment that appear to be most frequently employed. In Chapter Six there appears a review of ten additional tests or techniques. This chapter summarizes approximately fifteen additional tests which are frequently used in special education, psychology and regular education.

Detroit Tests of Learning Aptitude

The Detroit Tests of Learning Aptitude (DTLA) is a test of general learning aptitude consisting of twenty tests. The DTLA is recommended for ages three years to nineteen years. Out of the twenty tests, nine to thirteen are used to obtain an IQ for the child being tested. The tests contained in the DTLA consist of: pictorial absurdities; verbal absurdities, pictorial opposites; verbal opposites; motor speed, precision and auditory attention span for unrelated words and related syllables; oral commissions; social adjustments A and B; visual attention span for objects and letters; orientation; free association; memory for design; number ability; broken pictures; oral directions; likeness and differences; and totals.

In one review it is cited that in several areas the DTLA is inadequate. The first being that the DTLA is unsystematically standardized. Another weakness is that each test was given to only about fifty children to obtain an average score. This is not considered to be a representative number and leaves some doubt about the validity of the test.

The DTPA is graded on an individual basis, meaning that for each test a separate mental age is scored, thus making the score more useful to the teacher in the placement of the child and making the results of the test easier for parents to understand. When the parents see their child is talented in certain areas and below average in others they can more readily accept special help for the child than if they are simply told that their child is below average.

Utah Test of Language Development

The Utah Test of Language Development was developed by Merlin Mecham, Lorin Jex, and Dean Jones. This test provides an objective instrument for measurement of expressive and receptive verbal language skills in both normal and handicapped children. It not only provides a broad overall picture of expressive and receptive skills, but utilizes the developmental approach for appraisal of language readiness. Therefore, it should have special value as a tool for speech pathologists, audiologists, and the psychologists.

The Utah is easy to administer and the examiner can quickly become familiar with the rules and procedures concerning administration. Also, it is not a timed test and can be administered in more than one setting.

An additional advantage is the ease and rapidity with which the test can be given. It takes approximately thirty to forty-five minutes to administer.

Although it is not possible to diagnose the various basic elements of verbal language at the present time, a careful examiner can gain a great deal of insight concerning the various kinds of problems in language development with which the child is confronted. It affords the examiner a means of appraisal which can be utilized in studies of growth or change, individual differences, and exaggerated deviations such as one might find in those who are communicatively gifted or handicapped.

The test is approximately equally divided into items which measure selective and those which measure sequential language facility.

The validity of the Utah was checked by the method of calibration. It is felt that the test has good "face" validity. The age range for the Utah Test of Language Development is one to sixteen years.

It is the realization of the present authors that unrestricted use of the test as a diagnostic instrument is not feasible until a larger collection of normative data is available. It is with this idea in mind that the present test is being "launched" in its present form with the hopes that additional normative data will be forthcoming from users.

It is suggested that the test is satisfactorily reliable as an objective testing instrument.

Minnesota Preschool Scale

The Minnesota Preschool Scale, by Florence L. Goodenough, Katharine M. Maurer, and M.J. Van Wagenen tests the mental ability of young children. This test provides an estimate of verbal and nonverbal intelligence of children from six months to six years of age. The Minnesota Preschool Scale test is administered on an individual basis and takes less than thirty minutes to complete. Raw scores may be converted to IQ., percentile rankings or standard C scores. Reliability, validity and norming information are available from the publisher. The scale consists of assessing a child's ability by having him point to parts of the body, naming familiar objects, responding to pictures, obeying commands, discriminating forms, absurdities, speech, and others.

Ammons Full Range Picture Vocabulary Test

The Ammons Full Range Picture Vocabulary Test measures general intelligence as well as vocabulary comprehension. The APVT contains four pictures, which are shown to the child. As the examiner says a word, the child indicates which of the pictures best represents the given word. The APVT can be administered to a child as young as two years of age.

There is a shorter version of the Ammons Full Range Picture Vocabulary Test called the Quick Test. It is called the Quick Test because it requires very little time, between three and ten minutes per person to take the test. It was developed to be a very brief individually administered intelligence test. The QT uses a four-choice pictorial response format from which the testee has to point to the picture that "best fits" the given word. Only moderate training is required to give and score the QT. The items are arranged by difficulty. The QT uses a single plate of four pictures or scenes for all fifty items. In other words, each of the four pictures serves as the correct response for ten or so of the items. Three forms of fifty items each, each with an accompanying plate of four pictures are available.

Porteus Maze Test

This test came into being when Stanley Porteus was working with some retarded boys committed to a Boy's Home at Burwood, Victoria. The test consists of a series of line mazes of increasing difficulty. When the examiner uses the simpler mazes to demonstrate the process the test can be administered with no verbal instructions. The subject must trace with a pencil the shortest path from the entrance to the exit of the maze. There is no time limit. When the subject makes an error, he is stopped and given a second trial on an identical maze. If a second error is made, the examiner scores a failure at that level except at the highest levels where four trials are permitted. The mazes range in difficulty from the three year old level to an adult level. The Porteus Maze Test is part of the Arthur Point Scale and can be found in any of several different versions.

Currently the Maze test can be bought in three variations: original, extension and supplemental. Since its inception in 1914, the test has gone through quite an evolution. Because of these changes the test has achieved longevity and diversification.

The Goldman-Fristoe Test of Articulation

The Goldman-Fristoe Test of Articulation was designed by Ronald Goldman and Macalyne Fristoe to provide a means of assessing an individual's articulation of the consonant sound. This test can be used by a classroom teacher so he/she can learn whether or not a child is producing any incorrect sounds or to determine which sounds are misarticulated in a child's speech. The information can be used in referring the child for therapy. Information about the individual's articulation skills is obtained through three subtests. They are sounds-in-words, sounds-in-sentences, and stimulability.

The sounds-in-words subtest consists of 35 pictures that depict objects and activities that young children are familiar with. The child is required to name the pictures and to answer questions about them, giving this subtest a total of 44 responses. The purpose of this subtest is to permit the examiner to test the individual's spontaneous production of the English consonant sounds in their most common position. It also tests eleven consonant blends.

The sounds-in-sentences subtest has two stories which are read aloud by the examiner and is illustrated by sets of five and four pictures. The subject recounts each story in his own words, using the pictures as memory aids. This subtest has the potential for assessing most of the consonant sounds.

In the stimulability subtest, the individual is asked to watch and listen carefully as the examiner correctly produces the sound that the subject misarticulates. The subject then tries to repeat the sound he has heard. The stimulability is tested at all levels and the simplest level is the basic unit of speech, the syllable.

All materials in the Goldman-Fristoe Test of Articulation are contained in the Easel-Kit. The Easel-Kit is a compact device for displaying and storing the test materials. It was developed as the result of examination and experimentation with materials and methods used in articulation testing. This kit contains 35 pictures for the sounds-in-words subtest and nine pictures for the sounds-in-sentences subtest. The cards for the stimulability subtest are also located in it. There is also a supply of response forms and a test manual included.

When giving this test, the environment for administering it must be quiet, adequately lighted, and contain a table and two chairs or equivalent furnishings. The qualifications of the examiner depend upon which level of evaluation is to be attempted. The two levels are: (1) Each sound production is judged only for presence of error; and (2) Each sound production is judged for type of error. The test manual makes administering the test easy, even for the beginning examiner.

Test of Central Auditory Abilities

This is a test of auditory perception used in testing the auditory perceptual skills of young children and authored by Flowers and Costello. For early identification at the kindergarten and first grade level, the test identifies children with general auditory perceptual dysfunctions and establishes probabilities for future success in reading. For grades one through six, this test identifies the low achieving child. Certain low scores suggest specific learning disabilities which may be presumed to be interfering with the child's progress and learning.

The following features are what make the test a very comprehensive testing tool:

- The test requires the individual fifteen minutes test time.
- All test directions and practice items are on audio tapes.
- It has simplified scoring.
- It allows non-teachers (e.g. classroom aides) to administer the test, under supervision.

You do not use this test below 5.0 chronological age (CA) and it is not given to children at a grade level higher than sixth. This test is given on a one-on-one basis in a quiet room. It includes twenty-four items and nine trials. It is permissible to go through the trials several times. The test may also be used with other school populations such as: speech handicapped, mentally retarded, children with reading problems, educational and socially disadvantaged children, learning disabled children, children with language development problems, children with perceptually handicapping problems, and acoustically handicapped children.

Harris Test of Lateral Dominance

The Harris Test of Lateral Dominance is a sensory motor test, which has been used in speech and reading clinics for cases of disability, particularly when the problem of lateral dominance has been involved. This test consists of a twenty-seven page manual which has only five pages devoted to theory; the others are devoted to directions for administering the test. The test is interesting and relatively simple. Directions for administering and scoring the test and for interpretation of results are clear and complete.

The Harris Test of Lateral Dominance might be of value in the determination of laterality in cerebral lesions in adults with aphasia. One could also test pre-school children who have motor handicaps. Aside from its use in the reading disability and aphasia group, laterality testing will still be largely in the preschool age.

The author says the test was organized to meet the practical requirements of clinical practice and at the same time maintain satisfactory standards with regard to comprehensiveness, reliability and validity.

Boehm Test of Basic Concepts

The Boehm Test of Basic Concepts was developed by Ann E. Boehm. The BTBC is a picture test that was designed to specify the degree to which young children have mastered different concepts often found in materials used in pre-schools, and in first and second grade. This test is a valuable diagnostic and remedial tool. It strongly covers the areas considered to be sure targets for remediation. The BTBC does have grade norms, but it should mainly be used as a diagnostic inventory of the fifty basic concepts the test includes. The test can be given to small groups, but is often given individually. It may be given to kindergarten children and first and second graders. Administration usually takes about thirty minutes.

Walker Problem Behavior Identification Checklist

This test has a fifty item checklist and its purpose is the identification of children with behavior problems and is designed for use by the classroom teacher in the elementary grades.

A two month observation period is required. Five factors are involved in this test — acting out behaviors, withdrawal, distractibility, disturbed peer relations, and immaturity. Behaviors are observed and circled on a list of various behaviors listed. Included are: temper tantrums, rejection of school participation, defiance, anti-social behavior, verbal language — babbling, nonsense syllables, etc.

There are five subscores for each subgroup and the total of these gives the total scores. Because the initial test raw scores were positively skewed, they were converted into T scores. A T score of sixty, one standard deviation from the mean, is the separation point that divides the disturbed from the nondisturbed. A score of minus one and a half deviations from the mean would indicate a need for further evaluation.

Colored Progressive Matrices

One test which is relatively culture free is the Colored Progressive Matrices, which is designed by J.C. Raven. This test is used in booklet form today, but it was originally developed in "board-form," which was like a puzzle in which a design had to be completed. In the new booklet form, the person is shown a design with one part missing. The part missing is one-fourth of the design. There is a group of six parts pictured on the same page as the design. The person must select the right picture part to complete the design. Each design becomes progressively more difficult, so, it is suggested that this test may be used along with other tests to estimate the intellectual level. Because this test can be administered without verbal instruction or verbal responses needed it is said to be relatively culture-free. This test can be used with children and adults.

Test of Articulation

This test is designed to provide a systematic means of assessing an individual's articulation of the consonant sounds and was designed by Fristoe and Goldman. Articulation errors must be found before speech therapy is initiated. This test provides a guide for locating and recording articulatory errors in order to define problems for effective remedial services.

The Goldman-Fristoe Test of Articulation is designed to examine an adequate and accurate sample of the subject's speech production under several conditions ranging from imitation to conversational speech. It is presented in a form that is easy to administer and it eliminates loose cards and objects and can be presented in one test which contains all materials needed for testing and recording results.

The primary purpose of this test is to provide a method for testing that is simple enough for a teacher with a minimum of training to administer. It can be used by a classroom teacher to learn whether or not a child is producing sounds correctly and, if not, remediation procedures are in order.

CHAPTER 6

ASSESSMENT OF PERSONALITY AND ADAPTIVE BEHAVIOR

THIS chapter is different from the other chapters because in this chapter we are no longer dealing with behaviors but with interpretations of behaviors. It is true as Salvia and Ysseldyke (1978, p. 360) state, "adequate personality development and social competence are nebulous concepts, ill-defined and subjectively measured." We must evaluate behavior in children in terms of the degree to which it is disturbing and this is not limited to the person exhibiting the behavior but also includes the people who come in contact with that individual.

What behavior is acceptable and conforming? It would be difficult to think of any behavior that would be unacceptable universally. Salvia and Ysseldyke (1978, p. 360) tell us:

In various societies suicide is acceptable, homosexuality is openly practiced and condoned, aggressive language is expected. Within the majority culture of the United States, the same behaviors are interpreted differently, depending on the circumstances: total disrobing is an appropriate behavior before taking a bath; it is generally not considered appropriate behavior before being baptized. In wartime, taking a human life is sanctioned and even rewarded if the victim is an enemy soldier; in peacetime, the circumstances determine whether taking another's life is considered murder, manslaughter, or self-defense. Thus, the context and the circumstances determine in large part the evaluation of behavior.

PERSONALITY ASSESSMENT TESTS

In contrast with many other tests, projective tests have always been associated with personality assessment. They employ stories from ambiguous test stimuli to which the person is asked to respond or they might involve the child drawing pictures. We also employ personality inventories which are unlike projective tests in that they pose direct questions and limit the form of the answer such as requiring a yes/no response.

Psychologists also employ systematic observation of behavior in the child's natural setting. This enables the clinician to identify situational factors associated with patterns of unacceptable behavior. To discover a child's pattern of social behavior, for example, the clinician would observe him several times throughout the school day for several days.

Structured behavioral observation can also be employed by observing troubled families in family discussions and thereby learn about the patterns of interaction among family members.

Trained clinicians can also use a child's art work such as paintings, pictures, short stories, puppetry, etc., to assess personality deficits.

PROJECTIVE TESTS

Table 6.1 contains the most commonly used projective tests to assess personality deficits in children and some of them may also be used for adults.

Rorschach Inkblot Test

The Rorschach Inkblot Test is the most frequently used projective technique by clinicians. It was developed by Hermann Rorschach, a Swiss psychiatrist, in the 1920s, and quickly became a popular personality assessment tool in the United States.

Table 6.1

Commonly Used Projective Tests

Blacky Pictures (Blum, 1967)

Children's Apperception Test (Bellak & Bellak, 1965)

Draw-A-Person (Urban, 1963)

Holtzman Inkblot Technique (Holtzman, 1966)

House-Tree-Person (Jolles, 1971)

Human Figures Drawing Test (Koppitz, 1968)

Rorschach Inkblot Technique (Rorschach, 1966)

School Apperception Method (Solomon & Starr, 1968)

Thematic Apperception Test (Murray, 1943)

This test consists of a series of ten symmetric inkblots, some black and some white and some in color. The child or adult is asked to look at the card and tell the examiner what the inkblots make him or her think of. A set of characteristics called *determinants* are used to evaluate the responses. The determinants include color, form, movement, texture and depth. Responses are evaluated in terms of which portion of the card is explored, the subject matter of the response, total number, average time taken to respond to the cards, and the general behavior of the client during the evaluation.

The inkblots of the Rorschach possess considerable sentimental value for many psychologists, but the fact remains that a tremendous amount of research has generally failed to validate the Rorschach as one of the best diagnostic tools in personality assessment. As a matter of fact, the reliability of the various scoring systems has undergone tremendous criticism. The validity of the test has had little criticism because researchers, in general, feel that it is a well-designed projective technique. Holtzman's (1956) efforts to develop a better designed projective technique has led to a test without many of the shortcomings of the Rorschach.

EXHIBIT

Inkblot Facsimile

In a Rorschach test an inkblot like this is shown to persons; they are asked to respond in an open-ended way, telling the clinician what the inkblots look like. From their descriptions, clinicians make inferences about underlying drives, motivations, and unconscious conflicts.

Figure 6.1.

The Thematic Apperception Test

The TAT is a projective technique consisting of a series of vague pictures similar to those found in magazines. The client is asked to tell a story about what has happened in the past, what is presently happening, and what will happen in the future. Most of the pictures portray people in settings with some degree of vagueness. It is assumed that people respond to the pictures in terms of their own personality traits, motives, and desires. Henry Murray originally developed the test (Morgan and Murray, 1935); however, a great deal of credit should go to Bellak (1954). Bellak (1954, 1975) also developed a similar test for children, the Children's Apperception Test (CAT).

The TAT has four groups totaling thirty cards which are intended respectively for boys, girls, men and women.
Kleinmuntz (1967) reveals that studies, comparing the interpretations of the TAT, reveal a lack of widely accepted scoring criteria. Levels of scoring criteria are highest when raters are trained in similar interpretative techniques.

Meyer and Salmon (1984, pp. 75-76) state:
Thus, like most projective tests, the TAT appears to have at least some content validity despite reliability problems. Research conducted on the TAT indicates that the test is useful in assessing how clients would respond in situations that they perceive as similar to those depicted in the cards. The inference of constructs such as personality traits or fantasy activity is a much riskier undertaking.

Children's Apperception Test

The CAT is used with children from ages three to ten and consists of ten cards depicting vague stories utilizing animal figures. According to the manual accompanying the CAT (1961) it is stated that the original idea for the CAT came from Ernst Kris and was based on the supposition that children will identify themselves much more readily with animals than with persons. The manual written by Bellak and Bellak (1961) has this to say:

The C.A.T. was designed to facilitate understanding of a child's relationship to his most important figures and drives. The pictures were designed to elicit responses to feeding problems specifically, and oral problems generally; to investigate problems of sibling rivalry; to illuminate the attitude toward parental figures and the way in which these figures are apperceived; to learn about the child's relationship to the parents as a couple . . .

Children's Apperception Test — Human Figures (CAT-H)

The CAT-H was developed by Bellak and Bellak (1965) and is a human modification of the CAT. In constructing the CAT-H, humans were put into the vague pictures in an attempt to depict scenes which would elicit material relevant to important situations and problems in the child's life. It is believed by many that some children can identify better with human figures than animals although animals have the advantages of being more culture free and less structured. In the CAT-H manual by Bellak and Hurvich (1965) they state:

It is hoped that the CAT-H will usefully round out the armamentarium for the study of children. We still think of the regular CAT as the first instrument to consider. However, with children between seven and ten, and especially if their mental age is much higher than their chronological age, the CAT-H may often be more useful. In this sense the CAT-H may be a suitable bridge between the regular CAT and TAT.

PERSONALITY INVENTORIES

As already stated in this chapter, personality inventories pose direct questions to a person and the person being tested gives a short answer such as yes/no. There are a number of personality inventories available but three of the most widely used are the Cattell PF Personality Inventory, the California Personality Inventory, and the Minnesota Multiphasic Personality Inventory (MMPI). Of all the personality inventories, the MMPI is the one that is most used.

Minnesota Multiphasic Personality Inventory

Hathaway and McKinley (1943, p. 3) tell us that the MMPI was initially developed to aid in the differential diagnosis of psychiatric patients. These same authors state: "The chief criterion has been the valid prediction of clinical cases against the neuropsychiatric staff diagnosis, rather than statistical measures of reliability and validity." This means that the test was designed to produce a level of diagnostic accuracy which equals that of highly trained diagnosticians. The test is a long one, containing 550 true-false items, selected because they elicited maximum discrepancies between groups of psychiatric patients and normal subjects.

FIGURE DRAWINGS

Figure drawings are very popular and widely used in clinical practice as a quick method of assessing personality deficiencies.

There are several figure drawing tests on the market at the present time and the author will discuss three of the popular ones.

House-Tree-Person (H-T-P)

When administering the H-T-P the child is directed to draw a picture of a person, a tree and a house on three sheets of white paper. Jolles (1971) has a catalog for interpretation of the H-T-P. In this catalog Jolles (1971, p.9) makes a statement which he attributes to a man named Buck which says a lot about the use of the H-T-P.

> Buck emphasized the need to avoid attaching significance to an item unless the subject (S) has indicated that the item has significance to him: line quality, shading, proportion, comments, etc. He also cautions the clinician to avoid adhering strictly to general meanings of items because given items may not have such meanings to certain S's but rather have specific or idiosyncratic meanings. Finally, Buck stresses that an item may arouse positive as well as negative feelings in a S; once the S has demonstrated that an item has significance for him, the clinician must determine if this significance is positive or negative.

Jolles (1971, p.9) also makes another statement which is sound advice for not only the H-T-P but all projective tests:

> The H-T-P, like other projective techniques, is not a substitute for sound clinical training. A well-trained clinician will find the H-T-P technique — and this Catalogue — valuable, but one with meager clinical background will extract little from the H-T-P or this Catalogue.

Although Koppitz (1968) has done the most extensive research on human figure drawings, Machover (1949) was one of the pioneers in this area. Urban (1963) did extensive research. All three published Draw-A-Person Tests. In the preface of her book Koppitz has this to say about human figure drawings and the way children can express themselves:

> There has never been any doubt in my mind that of all tests and techniques used by psychologists, who work with children, there is one that is more meaningful, more interesting, and more en-

joyable than all others, and this technique is drawing, just drawing with pencil and paper. I know the value of drawing at first hand, having used it myself both as a child and as an adult to help me through periods of crises and inner turmoil. Drawing may involve "free drawing" of anything the child wants to depict, or the copying of designs, or the drawing of a specific topic at the request of the examiner, or the making of human figure drawings (HFDs). Even though I have watched hundreds and hundreds of children while they were drawing, I have never become bored and I keep on marvelling at the way boys and girls can express themselves and can reveal their attitudes through graphic images.

TESTS OF ADAPTIVE BEHAVIOR

Although several adaptive behavior scales have been briefly discussed in another chapter, the author would like to discuss in greater detail two of the most popular ones in our country.

AAMD Adaptive Behavior Scale and the ABS-PSV

Before discussing the AAMD Adaptive Behavior Scale and the Adaptive Behavior Scale—Public School Version, the author would like to write a segment about the assessment of adaptive behavior and adaptive behavior itself.

Adaptive behavior has been defined by the American Association on Mental Deficiency (Grossman, 1973) as behavior that is effective in meeting the natural and social demands of one's environment.

The assessment of adaptive behavior covers two major areas: The first area shows the person's ability in meeting independence needs. Secondly, how will the individual meet the social demands of his or her environment?

All of the definitions and explanations of adaptive behavior are important. But, a degree of vagueness is possessed by them. This is because there is no way of knowing the kinds of environments in which the individuals will be required to function. There is also no one instrument that can measure all of the necessary areas of adaptive behavior.

Primarily, adaptive behavior scales have been developed to provide information about handicapped individuals. They are helpful for the classification, treatment, and training decisions. An instrument used to measure adaptive behavior should never be the only criterion for evaluating an individual's adaptive behavior. Adaptive rating scales cannot be completely objective because behavior is viewed differently by teachers and parents, or whomever is observing the behavior. It is important that the informants credibility be evaluated.

The American Association on Mental Deficiency Adaptive Behavior Scale is used for institutionalized individuals. It is primarily used with mentally retarded, emotionally disturbed, and developmentally disabled individuals. It covers an age range of three to sixty-nine years. Two types of competencies are assessed—behavioral and affective. The scale is useful in evaluating the personal and social resources of the institutionalized individuals.

The test is divided into two parts. Part one is organized developmentally. It measures basic habits considered to be important to the maintenance of personal independence in daily living. Part two focuses primarily on maladaptive behavior related to personality and behavioral disorders.

The test takes approximately fifteen to thirty minutes to administer. Persons with little training can administer the test.

If only one person is giving the assessment, the person must be familiar with the individual. Interviewing the parents is most useful in assessment. More than one informant may also be used to obtain the desired information.

The standardization of the ABS was based on approximately 4,000 persons residing in sixty-eight facilities for the mentally retarded throughout the United States. The norms do not take into account differing cognitive ability levels (Sundberg, Snowden, and Reynolds, 1978).

The manual fails to provide test-retest reliability. The reliability and validity data is limited. It was recommended by several studies that neither placement decisions nor behavioral statements be made on the basis of ABC scores alone.

The AAMD Public School Version Scale aids in measuring the child's behavior level. It also helps to determine if remedial help in any of the areas of behavior is needed.

The ABS-PSV is similar to the ABS except for areas not applicable to behavior in the school setting. Those areas of the test were eliminated.

The ABS-PSV is administered in the same manner as the ABS version. It takes approximately fifteen to thirty minutes. The test is for children ages seven years, three months to thirteen years, two months. In order to have the most useful record, parents are encouraged to fill out the ABS-PSV as well as teachers.

The reliability of the ABS-PSV seems to be satisfactory but the validity is questionable for the population it is intended to serve.

Several studies have found that part two of the ABS-PSV may be inappropriate for certain groups of children. These groups include those who have physical handicaps such as deafness, blindness, or orthopedic difficulties. For children who showed evidence of emotional disturbance or those who had not the opportunity to learn the adaptive behaviors it was also inappropriate.

The ABS-PSV may be useful in evaluating children and developing possible education plans.

In closing, I would like to bring out again that this scale should not be the only criterion used in placement and evaluating an individual's adaptive behavior.

VINELAND SOCIAL MATURITY SCALE

The Vineland Social Maturity Scale (Doll, 1953) is a standardized tool that measures the level of social competence of an individual. The individual can be either normal or handicapped. The age range is from birth to maturity.

The scale has 117 items in order of increasing difficulty. The eight categories are: Self-help general, Self-help dressing, Self-help eating, Communications, Locomotion, and Occupation. In a child's case, the child's parent is used as an informant to obtain some of the information needed to complete the Scale.

The scale takes approximately twenty to thirty minutes to administer. The examiner should be qualified and have already devoted as much time as possible to mastering the technique. The scale is not a rating scale based on opinions, therefore, the informant does not make the scoring judgment.

In giving the examination, it is important to ask if the subject "usually does" instead of asking whether he "can-do" so-and-so. These answers are checked by detailed questioning until the examiner feels that he is able to score the item accurately. An example of detailed questioning is: "To what extent does Bobby do that?"

SCORING: A "+" is scored if it seems clear that the item is habitually performed. It is also given if the item is temporarily discontinued but could easily be re-established.

A "+F" is scored when the subject does not perform at the time of the examination because of special restraint, but did formerly perform successfully when there were no restraints.

A "+N.O." is given when the subject has not and does not now because of special restraint, but could learn quickly if these restraints were removed. "+N.O." scores receive full credit. They receive no credit within the range of continuous scores. They get half credit within the intermediate range. This means if the +N.O. score is the last of the continuous scores, then it is counted in the intermediate range and only gets half credit.

"±" is for those in transitional state, meaning they are occasionally performed. These are of half-credit value.

" – " is for those items which the subject performs rarely or under extreme pressure and receives no credit.

The total score is the sum of all the scores. This is done by adding to the basal score the credits beyond the basal for a total number. This score is converted to an age score from the values on the record sheet.

Overall, the Vineland is a useful instrument for providing information about social competence. It does, however, have its faults. It appears somewhat inadequate in the standardization procedure and also in psychometric properties. Also the standard errors of measurement are unknown which is a minus for any instrument of measurement.

BIBLIOGRAPHY

Bellak, Leopold: *The TAT & CAT in clinical use.* New York, Grune & Stratton, 1954.

Bellak, Leopold: *The Thematic Apperception Test, the Children's Apperception Test, and the Senior Apperception in clinical use,* 3rd ed. New York, Grune & Stratton, 1975.

Bellak, Leopold and Bellak, Sonya Sorel: *Children's Apperception Test.* Larchmont, New York, C.P.S. Inc., 1961.

Bellak, Leopold and Bellak, Sonya Sorel: *C.A. T.-H. Children's Apperception Test (Human Figures).* Larchmont, New York, C.P.S. Inc., 1965.

Bellak, Leopold and Hurvich, Marvin S.: *C.A. T.-H.: Manual.* Larchmont, New York, C.P.S. Inc., 1965.

Doll, Edgar A.: *Vineland Social Maturity Scale Condensed Manual of Directions.* Circle Pines, Minnesota, American Guidance Service, Inc., 1965.

Hathaway, S.R. and McKinley, J.C.: *Minnesotat multiphasic personality inventory: manual.* New York, Psychological Corp., 1943.

Crossman, H.J.: *Manual on Terminology and Classification in Mental Retardation.* Baltimore, Garamond Pridemare Press, 1973.

Holtzman, W.H.: The Holtzman inkblot technique. In A.E. Rabin (Ed.) *Introduction to modern projective techniques.* New York, Springer, 1968.

Jolles, Isaac: *A Catalog for the Qualitative Interpretation of the House-Tree-Person (H-T-P),* revised. Los Angeles, Western Psychological Services, 1971.

Kleinmuntz, B.: *Personality measurement.* Homewood, Ill., Dorsey Press, 1967.

Koppitz, Elizabeth Munsterberg: *Psychological Evaluation of Children's Human Figure Drawings.* New York, Grune & Stratton, 1968.

Machover, K.: *Personality projection in the drawing of the human figure.* Springfield, Charles C Thomas, 1949.

Meyer, Robert G. and Salmon, Paul: *Abnormal Psychology.* Boston, Allyn & Bacon, 1984.

Morgan, C.D. and Murray, H.A.: A method for investigating fantasies. The Thematic Apperception Test. *Archives of Neurology and Psychiatry, 34*:289-306, 1935.

Salvia, John and Ysseldyke, James E.: *Assessment in Special and Remedial Education.* Boston, Houghton Mifflin Co., 1978.

Sattler, Jerome M.: *Assessment of Children's Intelligence and Special Abilities,* 2nd ed. Boston, Allyn & Bacon, 1982.

Sundberg, N.D., Snowden, L.R., and Reynolds, W.M.: "Assessment of Personal Competence." *American Review of Psychology, 29*:179-229, 1978.

Urban, William H.: *The Draw-A-Person Catalogue for Interpretative Analysis.* Los Angeles, Western Psychological Corporation, 1983.

CHAPTER 7

SCHOOL READINESS

EDUCATORS agree that readiness for school entry involves a generalized readiness and refers to both academic and social readiness. We know that children differ widely in capacity, achievement, mental maturity, rate of development, emotional needs, as well as social needs. They all do not enter school at the same perceptual-motor development level, social level, with the same physical development, language development, same curiosity, motivational skills, and with a good self-image.

There is much readiness criteria written to establish guidelines, procedures, and techniques for determining school readiness. According to Salvia and Ysseldyke (1978), there are two different perspectives on readiness that determine how it is assessed. First, it should be viewed as the presence of the behavior, skills, and knowledge that are prerequisites to the mastery of skills information to be taught. Second, readiness can be viewed as the presence of certain processes such as intelligence, discrimination, and so on, that are believed to underlie the acquisition of the behavior or information to be taught.

These types of development and learning involve all aspects of the child, and necessitate discussion of the development of the whole child, for it is the entire child who goes to school — the entire child who succeeds or fails.

Acquiring readiness, like all learning, should be looked upon as a springlike developmental pattern and not as various items, content or experiences occurring at predetermined times. Each preparatory experience should travel toward a goal and at the same time push back to the first experience that forms the base. Each stage of readiness is a step toward the next stage, and all stages overlap.

At the present time more information from educational research and child development studies is available than ever before, concerning a child's early experiences and behavior and their significance in overall development. Many studies began in 1965 when President Lyndon Johnson announced that the federal government was going to do something about early educational failure. He signed a bill that established Head Start. It proposed that no child should enter the first grade seriously unprepared. Along with unprecedented expenditures of money and effort on preschoolers from low-income families, came dramatically increased support for all manner of research and service programs for children less than six years of age. Educational research began to flourish. The federal view of how to deal with educational underachievement focused on preventative programs for four-year-olds. After that preventative programs were extended down to three-year-olds and enrichment programs were added as supplements to the elementary schools.

Two years after President Johnson signed the Head Start bill, our research was teaching us that by the time a child reached three years of age, he had already undergone a great deal of education. It was found that in a group of twenty or thirty three-year-olds, there was likely to be at least one remarkably bright child. In their everyday behavior, these twenty or thirty three-year-old children showed the same pattern of special abilities found in outstanding six-year-olds. By 1968 educators were quite convinced that a long-term approach to understanding good development had to start with a focus on achievement during the first three years of life.

Educators and psychologists in their study on infants came to believe that the informal education that families provide for their children makes more of an impact on a child's total educational development than the formal educational system.

There is no doubt that each child is unique. Most can be educated in the regular classroom but about one out of every eleven has unique needs and requires special attention. Love (1972) has this to say about these special children who are not as ready for school as

89% of the childhood population:

> This means that educational opportunities should not be denied to any child. Also, it means that the potentialities for a child making a contribution to society are not a requirement for him to enter school. Education is for all, for each individual should be provided the best education according to his capabilities, whether it be in a special classroom or the regular classroom. We should have a commitment in America to every child, which includes those with vision, speech, hearing, and learning problems; those from disadvantaged backgrounds; and those who are gifted. There is no doubt that providing education for these children requires a variety of specialized skills and services, and also that they are costly and often necessitate radical innovation. Very often we must get away from tradition to do what is best for these children. What is best for these children can be done in the regular classroom but generally is not. This is why we now have and probably always will have special classes for exceptional children (p. 218).

Parents need to help their children develop the full range of human abilities in the early years of life. Educators believe that from this foundation of early experiences, the preschool child is ready to continue learning.

All aspects of the whole child must be at a certain culmination stage in order for that child to continue building his learning experiences after beginning formal schooling. It is true that each child will be at his own point of development once entering school; however, areas of readiness necessary for the child to function successfully in the normal classroom setting should be considered. The word *normal* is used because a child with a serious handicap cannot reach the achievement levels of a child with an intact central nervous system, no matter how good his early learning experiences were. The handicapped child will develop and achieve more slowly than the normal child, therefore the need for special considerations and provisions.

According to Thompson (1980), the child's first learning are motor and sensory and the child must be active on a motor level to develop knowledge. By the first three or four years of life, children typically have developed sufficient kinesthetic awareness to walk, run, and jump without constant supervision. Children must become aware of the large muscles and how to operate them. If a child has been inactive for a time during a stage of kinesthetic awareness, development of a certain gross motor activity, or movement, may not evolve. The child relies on visual control of movement and may never try to get back to kinesthetic control. Kinesthetic awareness continues to develop, but skills such as fine motor control (handwriting) are not usually well established until later in childhood. Motor development is certainly a criteria for school readiness, for movement is involved in all activities, whether it be movement of eye muscles or leg muscles.

Getman (1964), stresses the organismic basis of learning. He states that visual learning is responsible for approximately eighty percent of our acquired knowledge, and that when dealing with symbols and forms, the child must be able to perceive them correctly and interpret them adequately. He also feels that the perception of symbols is highly related to physiological development and has added a new dimension to the assessment of readiness. He stresses perceptual readiness and has organized an action program to develop it.

It seems appropriate to discuss here the two opposing views concerning the educability of intelligence, or the acceleration of the mental maturation in a child through school and home training. The first, known as the heredity view, hypothesizes that training cannot develop mental maturity faster than the child develops naturally. The proponents of this point of view believe that it is best to delay reading instruction until the child achieves sufficient mental maturity to begin reading. Alfred Binet, the originator of the intelligence test, was one of the first to use the phrase "the educability of intelligence." In 1909 he opened classes in France for mentally retarded children in an attempt to train their attention and reasoning abilities. Binet rejected the notion that "when one is dumb, one is dumb for a long time." On the other hand, proponents of the environmental viewpoint believe that the factors in intelligence which are required for reading are at least partly the product of early home and school training. In the view of these educators, it is best to establish a stimulating environment that will accelerate growth. These people believe that if this is done and mental maturity can be obtained earlier, then the teaching of reading can begin earlier. Both of these viewpoints have valid points and shall be considered by psychologists and educators.

This writer would like to state that it will be conclusively demonstrated in this chapter that children mature in the stages of development at different times. Individual differences, therefore, mean a great deal when one considers the learning process. Children should not all be given the same book in the first grade and told by the teacher, "children, we are going to learn to read." Some will not be ready to learn to read until they are nine years old chronologically. Many mentally retarded students will not be ready to read until they have chronological ages past nine. It takes a mental age of six years and six months to be mentally mature enough to learn to read. Because children differ in the level of readiness, grouping is a must in all school subjects.

Many studies have been done on reading readiness, specifically. Most do believe, as already stated, that chronological development of the whole child is vital for the child to learn good reading skills. The term readiness refers to a state of development that is needed before a skill can be learned. The term reading readiness, therefore, refers to the collection of integrated abilities and skills that the child must have in order to learn the complex process called reading. Kirk, Kliebhan and Lerner tell us that the important components of reading readiness are mental maturity, visual abilities, auditory abilities, speech and language development, thinking skills, physical fitness and motor development. Also important are social and emotional development, and interest and motivation. These factors comprise a system network in that they interact and interrelate with each other. Kirk, Kliebhan and Lerner present the following figure which presents these factors as a system, all of whose components are needed by the child to assure success in reading (*see* Figure 7.1, Kirk).

There are many kinds of readiness assessment devices used to assess a child's readiness for learning in school. Since intelligence or learning aptitude is believed to underlie all school subjects, it is the

A Systems Network of Components of Reading Readiness

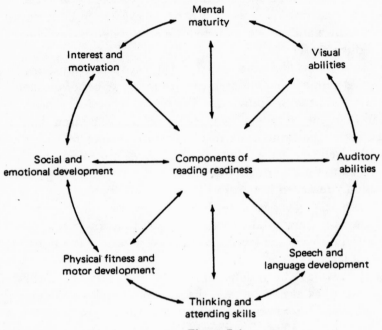

Figure 7.1.

most vital component of readiness assessment. General intelligence tests give global scores: either a mental age and I.Q. or both. Unless the subtests are analyzed, these global scores do not point out a child's major abilities and disabilities. Kirk, Kliebhan and Lerner (1978) tell us that tests of specific mental functioning are needed to show whether there are imbalances in mental abilities. Abilities and disabilities are measured by intra-individual tests, which measure specific kinds of functions.

Knowledge of a child's readiness will provide the teacher with invaluable information that may insure that the child enters an instructional sequence at an appropriate level. It can also provide the teacher with a destructive self-fulfilling prophecy that may actually hamper a child's development. Since decisions made on the basis of readiness tests are so important, the validity of the tests is crucial. It is evident that the academic development of children must be followed and documented. When one group of children are followed and their progress recorded, the data are called longitudinal. Readiness data must be longitudinal in both standardization and validity.

Naturally, reliability is a major consideration in evaluating the psychometric characteristics of any test. If a test is reliable and the tested trait or behavior is stable, a person will receive the same score on repeated testings.

The author has already discussed the many tests used for readiness in the schools of America. Needless to say, these tests are very useful and should be used with special care because much can be learned from the results of these instruments. Readiness for school is one of the most important facets of learning and should be a top priority thing when teaching the children of America.

BIBLIOGRAPHY

Getman, G.N.: The Physiology of Readiness, *Exceptional Children,* 41:251-255, 1964.

Kirk, Samuel A.; Kliebhan, Sister Joanne Marie; and Lerner, Janet W.: *Teaching Reading to Slow and Disabled Learners.* Boston, Houghton Mifflin, 1978.

Love, Harold D.: Attitudes Toward Special Education, *American Journal of Mental Deficiency,* 79:268, 1972.

Salvia, J., and Ysseldyke, J.E.: Assessment in Special Education, *Research on Teaching,* 57:183-189, 1976.

Thompson, M.: Head Start Teaches Lessons Board Members Should Learn, *American School Board Journal,* 6:167-170, January, 1980.

CHAPTER 8

WRITING PUPIL ASSESSMENT REPORTS

THE special education teacher receives information from many specialists such as psychologists, physicians, counselors, speech clinicians, etc. Often the special education teacher supplements this information and writes a pupil assessment report which is given to all the professionals who work with the child. The following report is an example of such an assessment report.

Jones School District
Jones, Arkansas

EDUCATIONAL ASSESSMENT REPORT

Identifying Information

Student's Name: _____Jane Marie Doe_____ Sex: ___F___

Age: _7 yrs, 9 mos_____ Evaluator: _Mary J. Kennedy___

Birthdate: _Jan. 6, 1976_____ Position: _L.D. Specialist___

Grade: _2nd_____ Parent: _Joe & Jane Doe___

Teacher: _Kay Smith_____ Address: _2 Oak St._____

School: _Jones Elem._____ Telephone: _555-0001_____

Referral: _Kay Smith, Teacher_ Date of Testing: _Oct. 24, 1983_

Background Information:

Jane was referred for a comprehensive psychoeducational evaluation to determine her eligibility to receive special education services.

Ms. Kay Smith, Jane's teacher, referred her for testing due to difficulty Jane had been experiencing in reading. Her teacher states that Jane has a great deal of difficulty in mastering phonics skills and in following written directions.

Jane attends the Metra Reading Program and her Metra tutor has expressed concern about Jane's reading difficulty.

The results of Jane's most recent group standardized (SRA) achievement test scores indicate that she was functioning at the 21st percentile in reading and the 90th percentile in math. Her present instructional levels are indicated as first grade in reading and second grade in spelling and math. Jane's attendance is average and she has passed all hearing and vision screenings conducted at her school by the school nurse.

Jane was rated by her classroom teacher on the Burks' Behavior Rating Scale. Those behaviors noted to a significant degree are indicative of poor academics and excessive dependency. Jane's teacher indicated it was difficult to rate Jane due to her very quiet nature.

Jane's mother provided the social and developmental history on her. Mrs. Doe indicated that she had several problems during and after her birth and that Jane weighed 5 pounds eight ounces at birth. Jane has allergies and takes medication for the allergies on a monthly basis. Other than allergies, Jane is in good health. Jane has repeated no grade and has received no special services.

Jane currently lives with her natural mother and father, and four older siblings; two of whom receive special education services.

Assessment

Intellectual Assessment

Wechsler Intelligence Scale for Children — Revised (WISC-R)
Verbal I.Q.: 82   Performance I.Q.: 117   Full Scale: 98

Subtests Scores:

Verbal		Performance	
Information	8	Picture Completion	9
Similarities	8	Picture Arrangement	12
Arithmetic	7	Block Design	15
Vocabulary	5	Object Assembly	11
Comprehension	9	Coding	15

Jane was given the WISC-R full battery. Her full scale I.Q. (98) indicated intellectual functioning within the average range. There is a significant (35 point) discrepancy between her verbal I.Q. (82) and her performance I.Q. (117).

On the verbal scale there is no significant scatter, but Jane's lowest subtest scaled score occurred on vocabulary. This indicates her expressive vocabulary development is on approximately a six year, two month developmental level.

Within the performance scale, there is a significant scatter. Jane's lower score occurred on picture completion, which is within the average range. Jane scored very high on block design and coding which indicated an aptitude for visual-motor integration skills.

Language Assessment

Peabody Picture Vocabulary Test—Revised (PPVT-R)
Standard Score: 68   Percentile: 2   Age Equivalent: 5-10

Jane's receptive vocabulary is in the extremely low range relative to her chronological age. Jane's receptive vocabulary development (5-10) is deficient as related to her expressive vocabulary development (6-2) as measured on the WISC-R vocabulary subtest.

Learning Processes:

Bender Visual Gestalt Test (Bender)
Koppitz Developmental Age: 9.0
Visual-Aural Digit Span Test (VADS)
Age Equivalent of Total VADS Test Score: 6.6—6.8

Visual Perception: According to the VADS subtests measuring visual perception skills, Jane's processing, sequencing and recall skills are below average. Visual input and visual with written expression were at the 25th percentile. Visual input with oral expression ranged from the 25th to 50th percentile.

Jane's Bender reproductions with a developmental age (nine years) exceed her chronological age which again indicate an aptitude for visual motor skills.

Auditory Perception: According to the VADS subtests on auditory perception, Jane has a significant deficiency in processing, sequencing and recall skills. Jane's aural input and aural input with oral expression were below the 10th percentile.

These findings on auditory perception coincide with those indicated by the discrepancy in the WISC-R Verbal and Performance I.Q.s. Those both suggest a difficulty in aural-oral processing and receptive/expressive language skills.

Achievement

Wide Range Achievement Test (WRAT)

Reading:	Grade Rating: 2.7	Standard Score: 90	Percentile 25
Spelling:	Grade Rating: 2.9	Standard Score: 95	Percentile 37
Arithmetic:	Grade Rating: 2.9	Standard Score: 94	Percentile 34

Woodcock Reading Mastery Test   Total Reading: Grade 2.3

Jane demonstrated skills in the areas of reading, spelling, and arithmetic resulting in scores within the average range on the WRAT achievement test. On the reading section, Jane's sight vocabulary was adequate to read silently during the test which suggests she processes better through visual modality without auditory feedback.

Observation:

Jane is an eight-year-old white female. She was tested at her school during two sessions on consecutive days.

Jane was attentive and cooperative throughout the testing. She showed no signs of particular interest in the test items. Jane tended to be very quiet and did not initiate conversation. Her responses to direct questions were often answered with short phrases, single word or non-verbal responses such as a shrug of shoulders or a nod of the head. Jane would sometimes say "I don't know" or "I can't do that."

Jane demonstrated a preference to use her right hand and had an acceptable pencil grip.

Jane's auditory and visual acuity are felt to be adequate and no physical problems were noted. The results of this evaluation are believed to be a valid assessment of her functioning level.

Summary and Impressions

Jane is an eight-year-old second grader of average intellectual ability. Jane exhibits the ability to function approximately at grade level in spelling and math. At this time she is experiencing a significant educational deficit in the area of basic reading skills (Woodcock).

This deficit is believed to be the result of a specific learning disability characterized by deficiencies in auditory vocal processing and/or receptive and expressive language difficulties.

Recommendations

1. Jane should be placed in a learning disability resource room for instruction in basic reading skills for sixty to ninety minutes a day.
2. Jane should be seen by the speech clinician weekly for structured instruction in developing receptive and expressive skills.

CHAPTER 9

PRESCRIPTIVE PROGRAM SETS DEVELOPED FROM CASE STUDIES — SAMPLE PSYCHOLOGICAL REPORT

A CASE study derived from school records, classroom observation and reports from certain specialists is a good source of information about a certain child.

The following four cases are presented but not in great detail. They are brief but show how information can be gained about a particular child.

Also, at the end of this chapter the reader will find a sample psychological report. Much information is included in the report and it is written in a manner that it should be helpful to the teacher.

CASE STUDY 1: MANUEL

Manuel is a ten-year-old Mexican boy of average size. His parents were born in Mexico, as were Manuel's older brothers and younger sister. For several years the father worked as a migrant farm laborer; therefore, the family moved around a lot.

School records indicate that Manuel started to school at age six, but missed three months of school that first year. During the four and a half years he has attended school, Manuel has missed about half. Records indicate that this little boy is presently reading at the third month of the first grade and working arithmetic at the fifth month of the first grade. Naturally, Manuel has a great deal of trouble with spelling and English usage.

Report from the School Psychologist

This specialist administered the Nebraska Test of Learning Aptitude by Marshall Hiskey which includes twelve sub-tests with pantomime directions. Manuel's Learning Age which is comparable to an intelligence quotient score was found to be 90. The school psychologist then got a Spanish speaking psychologist to administer the performance section of the WISC-R to Manuel and he scored an I.Q. of 105.

Needs Assessment Summary

Manuel is deficient in the English language and this includes phonology, morphology, syntax and semantics. Because of the language deficiency, he is also deficient in reading and spelling. He is adequate in math unless the problem must be read. Because of the findings of the school psychologist, Manuel is capable of overcoming his academic deficiencies.

Management Summary

Manuel should remain in the regular classroom but needs special help from specialists in language, reading, and arithmetic. In the regular classroom, Manuel should receive instruction in small groups and he should receive instruction on a one to one basis from the specialists.

CASE STUDY 2: MARIE

Marie was a ten-year-old girl. She was much smaller than other members of her class. She moved to Hawaii with her parents, three brothers and two sisters, from China when she was seven. Her parents worked in the sugarcane fields.

All classes were taught in English but her parents spoke no English. Several languages were spoken on the playground. Marie enjoyed playing and associating with other Chinese children, but upon returning to the classroom she was quiet and shy. She was polite and did not present a discipline problem.

The teacher was concerned that she did not achieve at a satisfactory level in reading, spelling and English. Her interest increased when it was time for art and she took great pride in copying from the chalkboard and books. In arithmetic she learned the addition, subtraction and multiplication facts, but could not work problems that she was required to read.

Report from the Education Examiner

The educational examiner administered the Harris-Goodenough Draw-A-Man Test and an individual non-language test, Form I of the Arthur Performance Scale. Results of these tests indicated average intelligence. A Chinese speaking psychological examiner administered the WISC-R to Marie. Her verbal I.Q. was 101, the performance I.Q. was 109 and the full scale I.Q. was 105, also indicating average intelligence.

Needs Assessment Summary

Marie was deficient in the English language which was the cause of her inability to achieve in academic subjects. Her parents spoke no English; therefore, the classroom was her only exposure to the English language.

It was decided that Marie's shyness was the result of her lack of association with individuals other than from her own race.

Due to Marie's small size it was decided that Marie felt inferior to other class members; therefore, she did not seek friends other than members of her own race which further limited her mastery of the English language. The family had limited income and could not afford a nutritional diet.

Summary

Due to Marie's deficiency in the English language and her small size, it was decided she should be retained in the same grade. A reading specialist and speech therapist would work with Marie on an individual basis. She would also be given remedial assistance in language and spelling. Her interest in art should be encouraged and she should be encouraged to use this talent in planned activities which would allow her to develop friendships with English speaking peers.

PSYCHOLOGICAL REPORT

As already stated, the following report contains a great deal of information which should be helpful to the regular class or special education teacher.

CONFIDENTIAL   **CONFIDENTIAL**

PSYCHOLOGICAL REPORT

Name of Student: Billy Johnson
School: Plainview Junior High
Chronological Age: 11 years 4 months
Mental Age: 7 years 6 months

Billy Johnson was administered the following tests at Plainview, Arkansas on June 10, 1984.

Wechsler Intelligence Scale for Children — Revised

	I.Q.
Verbal Score	64
Performance Score	72
Full Scale Score	66

Wide Range Achievement Test
    Word Recognition   2.7
    Arithmetic   2.6

Peabody Picture Vocabulary Test—Revised
    First Percentile

Bender Visual Motor Gestalt Test
Burks' Behavior Rating Scale
Love Oral Reading Test
Wepman Auditory Discrimination Test
    See Write-up

Billy was referred for psychological/educational testing because of low academic achievement. He was administered a battery of psychological/educational tests and the results are presented in the following paragraphs.

Psychological Assessment

Billy was administered the Wechsler Intelligence Scale for Children—Revised and had a Verbal I.Q. of 64, a Performance I.Q. of 72 and a Full Scale I.Q. of 66. He had a mental age of seven years, six months at the time of the testing. This places him in the educable range of mental retardation. He scored lower than average on all subtests with Information being the lowest and Picture Completion, Block Design, Object Assembly and Coding the highest.

Educational Assessment

Billy was administered the Wide Range Achievement Test and had word recognition skills at the seventh month of the second grade level, arithmetic skills at the sixth month of the second grade level, and spelling skills fell at the second month of the second grade.

Peabody Picture Vocabulary Test — Revised

On this instrument he scored at the first percentile. This means that ninety-nine percent of the children in the country score higher in language development and language knowledge than does Billy.

His receptive language age is seven years, six months.

Burks' Behavior Rating Scales

The Burks' Behavior Rating Scales (BBRS) are specifically designed to identify patterns of pathological behavior shown by children who have been referred to school or community counseling agencies because of behavior difficulties in the classroom or home. It is suitable for use with children in grades one through nine. The instrument is designed to be of assistance in the differential diagnosis of children already known to be in difficulty, but it is not suitable for routinely screening large groups of children who are performing adequately in school settings.

The BBRS is meant to be a preliminary device for identifying particular problems or patterns of problems a child may be presenting. It attempts to gauge the severity of negative symptoms as seen by outside persons—ordinarily teachers or parents. The 110 items used as criteria for the instrument's ratings describe behaviors that are infrequently observed among normal children.

According to the results of the Burks' Scales, Billy has trouble in the following areas:

1. Shows erratic, flighty or scattered behavior.
2. Is easily distracted, lacks continuity of effort and perseverance.
3. Gives inappropriate responses.
4. Attention span is short.
5. Shows poor vocabulary.
6. Is impulsive.
7. Homework is not done or incomplete.
8. Is rebellious if disciplined.
9. Is quickly frustrated and loses emotional control.

Examiner Impressions

Billy tried hard and gave a good effort. His low mental age was responsible for the low subtest scores. The examiner does feel that adequate rapport was established.

Bender Visual Motor Gestalt Test

The Bender-Gestalt is a test of visual-motor functioning and perceptual skills measured by the drawing of nine geometric figures. The test is intended to measure the process of visual-motor integration in children. It is used with students as a measure of observing approaches to visual-motor tasks and general assessment of fine motor skills.

The results of this instrument indicate that Billy has a moderate visual/perceptual/motor problem. This problem is severe enough to interfere with his ability to read, write and see things as a whole. The inability to see parts made into a whole will also affect other academic areas. Billy's perceptual age equivalency was six years, eight and one-half months at the time of the evaluation.

Love Oral Reading Test

This is a test to measure a child's reading comprehension. The child reads a paragraph aloud while the examiner marks the mistakes made by the child. Finally, a comprehension level is reached by the child and the examiner makes a note of this level. He had eight gross mispronunciations and one partial mispronunciation. He also had one omission, no insertions, one substitution, fifteen repetitions and had to be aided ten times. The examiner observed that he was unaware of errors, read word-by-word and disregarded the punctuation. He reached his reading comprehension level at the third grade.

Wepman Auditory Discrimination Test

Wepman's research indicates that there is a very high correlation between auditory discrimination and reading ability. If a child has inadequate development in auditory discrimination he needs particular help in this area. Inadequate development is shown by the following scores:

For 5 year olds, errors greater than six.
For 6 year olds, errors greater than five.
For 7 year olds, errors greater than four.
For 8 year olds, errors greater than three.

Billy had ten errors.

Recommendations

It is recommended that Billy be placed in activities that will enable him to compensate for his lack of background experiences. This will involve exposing him to a wide variety of objects and having him identify their purposes and functions. Also, he should be given the opportunity to acquire a number of facts such as learning the names of the months, how many weeks are in a year, etc.

It is recommended that Billy be assigned to either a resource room or to a class for the educable mentally retarded, with preference being given to the one that is the least restrictive. The basis for this recommendation is Billy's need for individualized instruction and his need to be in a classroom environment where he can compete with his peers on a more equal basis.

It is recommended that Billy be involved in activities that will improve his ability to group objects on the basis of a property that is common to them. Included would be activities ranging from grouping objects on the basis of shape (round objects in one group, square objects in another, etc.) to using words to classify objects (a chair and a table are pieces of furniture).

Billy is weak in listening skills and the following recomendations will help him in this area. The teacher should read a sentence to Billy. Have him repeat it several times until he has it memorized. Use sentences such as "The boy ran up the hill." Read sentence omitting one word or more and have Billy complete the sentence.

1. The _____ ran up the hill.
2. The boy ran up the _____.
3. The boy ran _____ the hill.
4. The boy _____ up the hill.

It is recommended that Billy be given instruction that will improve his skills in arithmetic. The following are examples of procedures that can be used:

1. Where necessary, review and reinforce primary skills.
2. Teach concept of odd and even numbers. Concrete objects may be used.
3. Introduce the concept of halves and quarters (simple fractions). Flannel board materials, blocks and pie cut outs may

be used for demonstration.

4. Extend numerical concepts such as equalities and inequalities, addition and subtraction facts through one hundred number families. Concrete objects may be used for demonstration. Drill and practice of facts are essential.

Student eligibility for special education is certified by the establishment of the primary handicapping condition of educable mental retardation.

School Psychologist

CHAPTER 10

PSYCHOLOGICAL EVALUATION OF PHYSICALLY HANDICAPPED AND NON-VERBAL CHILDREN

WE have a test standardized on deaf children, Nebraska Testing of Learning Aptitude (NTLA, Hisky, M., 1966, Psychological Corporation). We also have tests for blind children, Blind Learning Aptitude Test (BLAT), Newland (copyrighted by T. Ernest Newland), the Hayes-Binet (a special form of the Stanford-Binet that is used with blind children) and the Haptic Intelligence Scale for Adult Blind (an adaptation of the performance section of the WAIS, Shurrager and Shurrager, Psychological Research). In this chapter the author wishes to discuss tests which can be adapted for the physically handicapped and non-verbal scale.

The rehabilitation of physically impaired students has increasingly concerned psychologists and educators during the past decade. The appropriateness and quality of the services these students receive are as important as the number of individuals receiving these services, if true rehabilitation is to occur. In planning programs for this population, it must be remembered that while physical disabilities handicap an individual, poor self-concepts that sometimes accompany these disabilities can be as crippling as the handicap itself. Too, physical handicaps are often medical problems

---

Most of this chapter is adapted from the following work: Love, Harold D., "Psychological Evaluation of Physically Handicapped Students." *PRISE reporter*, no. 13, April 1982.

that prove to be psychological and educational barriers as well. These complexities mean that if physically handicapped students are to be rehabilitated, their educational programming must stem from psychological and educational testing that allows for these perplexities, and is therefore valid.

All testing with the physically handicapped must take into consideration the individual's ability to see, speak, hear, write, or otherwise respond to directions. The severity of the disablement influences test results; therefore, the examiner must be well versed in the performance of the non-handicapped on identical tests. The selection of suitable tests is determined by the examiner in instances where speech and motor dexterity are present. The subject's verbal comprehension may influence the selecting of a test. Modifications in administering standard tests become necessary when the more than moderately physically involved individual is present.

When discussing the psychological evaluation of children with physical handicaps, it must be noted at once that this group is large and has commonly divergent characteristics. The causes of handicaps are many, and the results vary according to the cause. The primary concern in evaluating these children is that tests and measurements are set up for and standardized on a group of children representing the normal curve. Because handicapped children undeniably have physical problems, in many cases (particularly with such problems as cerebral palsy) at least a chance of neurological impairment exists.

One of the greatest problems when testing handicapped children and interpreting the results is that one cannot be sure whether a low score on an intelligence test is a result of low intelligence, poor reading ability because of the child's handicap, or sensory defects which accompany the physical handicap. If the child is being treated with anticonvulsant drugs, this may be a distorting factor in his or her test performance. It is also important to remember that perceptual and spatial disabilities occur frequently in certain kinds of cerebral palsy, and that these are not necessarily reflective of overall intellectual level.

Few individual intelligence tests can or should be administered by classroom teachers. One of the basic assumptions underlying psychoeducational assessment is that, because of their complexity, the person who uses tests is adequately trained to administer, score, and interpret them. Such tests should be used only by licensed or certified psychologists, who have specific training in their use.

Individually administered intelligence tests are most frequently used for making educational placement decisions. State special education standards typically specify that data about intellectual functioning must be included in placement decisions and that these data must come from individual intellectual evaluation by a certified psychologist.

Many physically handicapped children have additional handicaps (for example, blindness, deafness, or perceptual problems) that interfere with their ability to respond to traditional general intelligence tests. This fact has led several test authors to develop individually administered tests designed to assess the intelligence of physically handicapped and multiply handicapped persons.

The author believes that if a physically handicapped student has moderate to severe hands and arms involvement, the best assessment of intelligence would be the Verbal Section of the Wechsler Preschool and Primary Scale of Intelligence (WPPSI), copyrighted in 1963 and 1967; the Verbal Section of the Wechsler Intelligence Scale for Children — Revised (WISC-R), copyrighted in 1974; or, the Verbal Section of the Wechsler Adult Intelligence Scale — Revised (WAIS-R), copyrighted in 1981. If the student does not have a hand involvement and his or her speech is relatively clear, the Verbal and Performance Sections of all three of these tests can be administered. The WPPSI can be administered to children from three years, ten months and sixteen days to six years, seven months and fifteen days of age. The WISC-R can be administered to children six years, zero months to sixteen years, eleven months and thirty days of age. The WAIS-R can be administered to individuals ranging in age from sixteen through seventy-four.

The Stanford-Binet Intelligence Scale is the grandfather of all intelligence tests. The original scales were developed by Alfred Binet in 1905 in collaboration with Theodore Simon. In 1908 the scale was revised by grouping items according to age, and the concept of mental age was introduced. The Binet-Simon Scale was revised in 1911, and in 1916 Lewis Terman revised and extended the scale for use in the United States. The 1972 edition of the Stanford-Binet is the third revision of the test and was developed by renorming the 1960 edition.

The Stanford-Binet can be used with physically handicapped children who have minor limitations to the same extent that the Wechsler series can be used. There are verbal subtests and performance subtests; however, the test is not broken down into a verbal section and a performance section. Therefore, the examiner must be careful in selecting the subtests administered to a physically handicapped child. The author believes that the Wechsler Scale is more adaptable for evaluation of the physically handicapped than is the Binet.

The Slosson Intelligence Test (SIT), published in 1971, is a relatively short screening test designed to evaluate mental ability. The SIT is a Binet-type scale that includes many items that appear in the Stanford-Binet Intelligence Scale. Since it does not require interpretation by the examiner, this test can be administered by teachers, counselors, or psychologists with the assistance of a second professional who knows the child extremely well. The administrator of the test uses the person who knows the child extremely well to answer most of the questions for the child. Therefore, a mental age can be obtained for a physically handicapped child, even though he or she has limited or no speech and has severe motor involvement.

While age ranges for individuals who may be tested are not specified, Slosson items range from the five month to the twenty-seven year level. Although the test was standardized on an unspecified sample, and information about its technical adequacy is limited, it does provide a broad sample of behaviors and can be valuable in screening physically handicapped children for more in-depth psychological evaluations.

Another test that can be used to screen physically handicapped children is the Goodenough-Harris Drawing Test. If this psychological tool is used, the child must have adequate use of the dominant or both hands. This test can be used with children ranging in age from three to fifteen years. It is a non-verbal test of mental ability suitable for use as either a group or individual test. Dr. Hale Harris restandardized the Goodenough Draw-A-Man Test and also standardized a similar Draw-A-Woman scale. At the present time, there is an experimental self-drawing scale being studied. It should be mentioned again that this test, which takes between five and fifteen minutes, should be used only for referring physically handicapped children for additional psychological testing.

There are a number of picture vocabulary tests that use receptive vocabulary as a means of assessing children's intelligence. Almost all of these can be modified to test the vocabulary knowledge of physically handicapped children. The tests are not measures of global intelligence; rather they measure only one aspect of intelligence—receptive vocabulary. There is, however, a high correlation between vocabulary knowledge and general intelligence. These tests should not be used to make placement decisions except when the results are corroborated by other psychological tools that measure more than one aspect of intelligence. Although there are many such tests (Full Range Picture Vocabulary Test, Quick Test), the author prefers the most up-to-date picture vocabulary test, i.e., the Peabody Picture Vocabulary Test—Revised (PPVT-R), which was published in 1981.

The PPVT-R can be administered to a child who is able to point to a picture, touch a picture, or in some way communicate to the examiner or a third individual which picture represents the word. While four pictures are shown to the child, the examiner pronounces a word and the child points to or touches one of the pictures. The mental age is obtained in the revised Peabody and there is an age equivalent which correlates with the mental age, and also a standard age equivalency which correlates with the intelligence quotient.

One of the author's students devised an instrument that was a board divided into four parts with a light in each part. When the four pictures were presented to the physically handicapped student, he or she could touch the section of the board that represented the word. When this particular section was touched, a light would come on, indicating the numbers 1, 2, 3 or 4. The board could fit on a wheelchair, be placed on a table, or put on the floor. The child could touch the four sections of the board with his or her finger, hand, elbow, chin, head, feet, or toes.

The author has mentioned many tests that could be adapted for the physically handicapped student, but one must always realize that adaptations take place. The author would prefer, however, to utilize the Peabody Picture Vocabulary Test—Revised as a screening device, and to follow this with the Full Scale Score of one of the Wechsler tests or the verbal sections of one of the Wechsler tests. In his opinion, this would be the best method for obtaining the intelligence quotient of the physically handicapped student. Other tests mentioned in this chapter would help in the psychological writeup and in the assessment of the child who is handicapped by physical limitations.

Alternative Testing Procedures for the Non-Speaking Student

Testing the severely physically handicapped student is a challenge for the most skilled evaluator. With the non-speaking student, ways of assessing verbal expressive skills using norm referenced instruments are limited. Alternative systems, such as fingerspelling, manual communication, or language boards using printed symbols or letters, may provide a means of communication. The effectiveness of these systems, however, depends on the efficiency of their delivery and the ability of the examiner to interpet them. Above all, alternative systems are often limited to the familiar lexicon that is used by the student in daily interactions. For these reasons, language-free instruments, like the Columbia and Leiter, are often chosen over the more preferred Binet L-M and WISC-R which are used with non-handicapped populations.

Suggestions from recent literature include using modifications such as yes/no responses to verbal questions, multiple choice tasks for vocabulary comprehension and association tasks, and encoding techniques in place of items requiring a verbal response. While these modifications facilitate gathering useful information on the child's receptive language comprehension, they do not adequately represent his or her full range of expressive competence.

A portion of this chapter is adapted from the following work: Territo, Jackie, "Alternative Testing Procedures for the Nonspeaking Student." *PRISE reporter*, no. 13, April, 1982.

Those students whose primary means of expression is through written language, and who have achieved competence in written communication, may have this option available to use in formal diagnostic testing.

At Pioneer Education Center, a Pittsburgh Public School, alternative communication devices provide another response mode for the nonspeaking student. Using a Canon Communicator (a portable printing device), one student recorded his verbal responses to the WISC-R and obtained a full scale I.Q. when he was tested by the school psychologist. His test scores reflected receptive and expressive intelligence, and the printed copy provided a lasting copy of responses for future reference. Subtests of ITPA (Auditory Sequential Memory, Auditory Association, Grammatic Closure, Sound Blending, and Auditory Closure) were also completed using portable printing devices.

Other systems which could be used similarly include: Sharp Memowriter, Personal Microcomputer with Printer, and a scanning printer such as the Zygo 100 and Zygo printer. The VIP by Prentke Romich and the Micon MCM could also be used to immediately display responses, but they do not offer hard copy. Improved methods of assessment offer the multiply handicapped a more equitable opportunity to prove their abilities on standardized diagnostic tests.

INDEX

121